Couples Counseling

Techniques, Ideas and Tips for Those Looking to Rekindle the Strength and Resilience Back Into their Relationship; the Key to Respect, Love & Joy

Erica May

any other individual or persons for any purpose other than that for which it was initially intended. It is strictly prohibited to amend, reproduce, distribute, utilize, quote, or paraphrase any part of the content within this publication without prior authorization from the writer or publisher. Any violation of these regulations may result in legal action against those who have breached them.

Disclaimer Notice

The presented work is strictly informational and should not be interpreted as an offer to buy or sell any form of security, instrument, or investment vehicle. Furthermore, the information contained herein should not be taken as a medical, legal, tax, accounting, or investment recommendation given by the author(s) or any affiliated company, employees, or paid contributors. In other words, the information is presented without considering individual preferences for specific investments regarding risk parameters. General information does not account for a person's lifestyle and financial objectives. It is important to note that no tailored advice will be provided based on the given information.

Table of Contents

CHAPTER 5: SERENITY TOGETHER: MINDFULNESS AND STRESS MANAGEMENT 65

CHAPTER 6: THERAPY AS A TOOL: PROACTIVE VS. REACTIVE APPROACHES 76

CHAPTER 7: FROM CONFLICT TO COMPASSION:

Welcome to the

Ideas Worth Sharing

Series

My name is Nicholas Bright, and I've spent nearly two decades working as a psychologist specializing in Behavioral Neuroscience and Interpersonal Communication in the US, UK, and Australia. Throughout my career, I've encountered countless stories, experiences, and insights that have shaped my understanding of the human mind and interpersonal interactions.

This series is a collaborative effort, bringing together the experience and expertise of myself and my colleagues: Erica May, Jeff Sharpe, Camila Alvarez, and potentially new faces in the future! We've chosen to write under pen names to respect everyone's privacy and keep the spotlight on the valuable content we offer rather than us as individuals. This decision allows us to freely share our knowledge without the distractions that often come with the limelight. We stand by the authenticity and credibility of the content shared here—our professional integrity remains at the forefront of this series.

We are deeply passionate about our field, and our primary goal is to equip you with practical, research-backed insights that you can implement in your everyday life. Each chapter is designed to inspire and help you better understand yourself and those around you.

We invite you to engage actively with the material: take notes, discuss the ideas with friends and family, and, most importantly, apply the lessons in your daily routine.

1. **Read;** understand what can be done to improve
2. **Reflect;** appreciate your feelings and their origins
3. **Remember;** put your learning into action

Thank you for embarking on this journey of knowledge and growth with us,

Nick

Want to Win Free Books?

Join Our Newsletter!

In this series, we appreciate that someone may find many different books helpful. I certainly know that when discussing sensitive topics like, for example, divorce, we can end up working on grief, anxiety, self-confidence, cognitive dissonance, and lots more. When we encounter a major challenge in life, it is rarely due to one small problem but rather a concoction of our experiences, outlooks, and actions; it's often a deep-rooted issue with many different things we need to uncover and support. We are complicated beings, and we must recognize this. As such, I would love to invite you all to join our newsletter.

In this, I aim to write articles of interest, including excerpts from various books in the series, as well as **vouchers**, **discounts**, and **giveaways**—and of course, no gimmicks or catches. I harbor a deep loathing of companies that offer seemingly amazing deals, only to charge you vast amounts in hidden fees! I vowed to never fall into that trap myself, and any offers I make are designed to be of true benefit and help. If you win a book in a giveaway, I want you to read it with a smile.

Join our newsletter and discover the additional value we can add to your life's curriculum!

Join us at: **www.IdeasWorthSharingSeries.com/newsletter**

See you on the inside!

About the Author: Dr. Erica May

Dr Erica May is a dedicated Clinical Psychologist practising in New York City. She graduated from Syracuse University in New York State, earning her degree in Clinical Psychology. Erica specializes in Cognitive Behavioral Therapy (CBT), Dialectical Behavior Therapy (DBT), and trauma-focused treatments. Her work is deeply rooted in helping individuals navigate complex emotional landscapes, enabling them to lead healthier and more fulfilling lives. Her compassionate approach and expertise have garnered her a reputation as a trusted mental health professional in her local community.

Erica has been friends and has worked with Nicholas Bright, the lead author of the Ideas Worth Sharing series, for many years. Together, they aim to help support a wider community by writing a book series on important topics within Psychology and extending their therapeutic insights and techniques beyond the confines of their practice. This book series will cover various topics related to mental health, including detailed guides on implementing CBT and DBT strategies in daily life, as well as comprehensive approaches to prevention, understanding and healing. By presenting practical exercises and learning through her practice, Erica hopes to make evidence-based psychological concepts more accessible to a broader audience. She aims to empower individuals with the knowledge and tools to manage their mental health proactively and independently, fostering greater resilience and well-being.

Preface

"The greatest happiness of life is the conviction that we

are loved; loved for ourselves, or rather,

loved despite ourselves."

Victor Hugo

This book is an ode to every couple who strives to breathe new life into their relationship, seeking deeper understanding and a richer connection. It bridges professional couples therapy techniques and daily interactions, aiming to demystify the complexities often associated with counseling. Through its pages, you'll discover how to enhance communication, resolve conflicts effectively, and foster intimacy practically and profoundly.

I was inspired to write this book after witnessing many friends and acquaintances struggle with their intimate relationships. They often shared how they felt lost in translation with their partners, with the love that once seemed so vibrant now muffled under layers of misunderstandings and unmet expectations. Their stories resonated deeply, reminding me of my past relationship challenges. This connection to the issues has fueled my passion to offer theoretically sound and richly applicable guidance.

The insights gathered here are drawn from personal experiences and scholarly research. I am deeply grateful to my mentors in psychology and therapy, whose wisdom has been instrumental in shaping the perspectives shared in this book. Their commitment to improving relationship dynamics has been a constant source of inspiration.

Thank you, the reader, for choosing to embark on this journey with me. Your willingness to explore new dimensions of your relationship is commendable. This book is written for proactive individuals—whether newly engaged or in long-standing partnerships—ready to peel back the layers of their interactions and build a stronger, more loving connection with their significant other.

The strategies outlined here are designed to be straightforward and actionable. By integrating these practices into your daily life, you can expect to see tangible improvements in how you and your partner relate to each other. Imagine expressing your deepest feelings without fear of misunderstanding or conflict and receiving emotional support that elevates your everyday experience.

As we proceed, remember that every step forward is towards a more fulfilling partnership. I invite you to turn the page and discover the keys to rekindling the connection in your relationship. Embrace this opportunity to transform your communication and the essence of your intimacy.

Introduction

"Love is not about how many days, months, or years

you've been together. Love is about how much

you love each other every single day."

Unknown

In a world where relationships are often tested by external pressures and internal dynamics, understanding the intricacies of maintaining a healthy partnership is more vital than ever. This book is designed to serve as a comprehensive guide for couples striving to enhance their connection, navigate conflicts, and build a resilient relationship foundation. It offers practical tools, strategies, and insights to foster deeper communication, intimacy, and mutual understanding.

Often, couples are stuck in repetitive cycles of miscommunication and unresolved conflicts. This guide breaks down these barriers by introducing effective communication techniques that can transform how partners interact. By learning to express needs clearly, actively listen, and empathize, couples can uncover the root causes of their issues and address them more constructively.

Conflict, while inevitable, does not have to be detrimental to a relationship. This book demystifies conflict resolution by framing it as a collaborative rather than a combative one. You will discover methods for approaching disagreements with a solutions-oriented mindset, ensuring that both partners' perspectives are respected and valued. These techniques will empower you to turn potential disputes into opportunities for growth and understanding.

Intimacy is another cornerstone of a thriving relationship, extending beyond physical connection to emotional and intellectual bonding. This book explores ways to enhance intimacy, emphasizing the importance of shared experiences, open dialogue, and vulnerability. By cultivating intimacy on multiple levels, couples can create a holistic bond that is robust and enduring.

Throughout these pages, you will find real-world examples and practical exercises to help you apply the principles discussed. These actionable steps are intended to bridge the gap between theory and practice, enabling you to see tangible improvements in your relationship dynamics. Whether you're a couple in crisis or simply looking to strengthen an already solid partnership, the strategies outlined here are adaptable to various situations and challenges.

Moreover, this guide highlights the importance of ongoing relationship maintenance. Just as we invest time and effort into our physical health, so should we commit to the health of our relationships. Regular check-ins, dedicated time for connection, and a proactive approach to addressing issues can prevent minor problems from escalating into significant conflicts. Couples can build a sustainable, loving partnership by making relationship care a continuous priority.

The journey to a revitalized relationship begins with taking the first step—acknowledging the need for change and being open to new approaches. This book encourages couples to move from passive contemplation to active participation in their relational well-being. The goal is not to achieve perfection but to make consistent progress towards a stronger, more fulfilling partnership.

While this book thoroughly explores couples therapy techniques, it also acknowledges the limitations of self-help. Every relationship is unique, and what works for one couple may require adaptation for another. Additionally, some deeply entrenched issues may benefit from professional counseling beyond the scope of this guide. Therefore, this book should be used as a complement to, rather than a replacement for, professional support when needed.

As you embark on this journey, remember that change is a process that requires patience, commitment, and love. Integrating the strategies and insights offered here into your daily interactions will enhance your relationship and empower you to manage and resolve conflicts confidently. The true measure of progress lies in the strength of your connection, the depth of your understanding, and the resilience of your love.

Ultimately, this book aims to provide you with the tools and knowledge to navigate the complexities of your relationship. Embrace this opportunity to grow together, and let each challenge you face be a stepping stone towards a deeper, more meaningful connection.

Chapter 1: Myth-Busting Therapy: Beyond Quick Fixes

"A great relationship doesn't happen because of the love

you had in the beginning, but how well you

continue building love until the end."

Unknown

Dispelling the Myths: The Real Journey of Couples Therapy

When stepping into the world of couples therapy, many bear the weight of misconceptions—beliefs that therapy is a magic fix or a last-ditch effort to save a relationship teetering on the brink of collapse. However, these myths can cloud the true purpose and potential of therapy, setting couples up for unrealistic expectations and potential disappointment. This chapter clarifies the fog surrounding couples therapy, emphasizing its value as a remedial and preventative tool in nurturing relationships.

Couples therapy, contrary to popular belief, is not just for relationships that are facing severe crises. It is also a strategic approach for couples looking to deepen their connection and prevent future discord. By understanding what therapy entails—a progressive journey rather than an immediate cure—couples can better prepare themselves for what is a commitment to mutual growth and understanding.

Common Misconceptions About Couples Therapy

The idea that couples therapy provides instant solutions is one of the most pervasive myths. Instant results are unrealistic and undermine the true essence of therapy, which is to foster gradual change and development. Couples must recognize that lasting improvement comes from consistent effort over time, not overnight.

Another widespread myth is that therapy is only meant for resolving major conflicts or saving a relationship from imminent dissolution. This chapter will clarify that therapy can also serve as preventive care. By engaging in therapy proactively, couples can fortify their relationship against potential challenges, enhancing communication and intimacy before significant issues arise.

Setting Realistic Expectations

A fundamental part of this therapeutic journey involves setting realistic expectations. Understanding that progress typically occurs over months rather than days or weeks can significantly alter how couples engage with the process and each other. This realistic perspective helps maintain motivation and commitment when quick fixes are not apparent.

The Dual Role of Therapy

Recognizing the dual role of therapy—as both preventive and corrective—can revolutionize how couples view their relationship maintenance strategies. When couples embrace therapy as part of their regular relationship health regimen, they open up new pathways to understanding and supporting each other in everyday life.

Throughout "Love Revived," we will explore various techniques and strategies to effectively communicate needs, resolve conflicts amicably, and build intimacy. These tools are designed to help during trouble and enrich the relationship's day-to-day dynamics.

By demystifying what couples therapy can realistically achieve, this chapter sets the stage for a deeper exploration into how targeted communication strategies and deliberate emotional connections can lead to a fulfilling partnership. The journey through counseling is depicted not as a series of quick fixes but as an evolving process where both partners learn and grow together, enhancing their overall relationship quality.

In summary, this chapter prepares readers to embark on a transformative journey beyond crisis management by busting common myths about couples therapy, setting appropriate expectations, and recognizing its comprehensive benefits. It invites them into a proactive stance towards nurturing their relationship, ensuring they understand that this process is about continuous improvement rather than instantaneous solutions.

Misconceptions about couples therapy often hinder individuals from seeking help or fully engaging in the process. One prevalent myth is the expectation of immediate results. Therapy is not a magical cure that transforms relationships overnight; it is a gradual process that requires both partners' time, effort, and commitment. Unrealistic expectations of instant changes can lead to disappointment and premature abandonment of therapy. Understanding that sustainable growth and improvement in a relationship take time to cultivate is crucial.

Another common misconception is that therapy should only be sought as a last resort in times of crisis. Therapy is not solely for relationships on the brink of collapse; it can be a valuable tool for enhancing communication, addressing underlying issues, and fostering deeper intimacy, even in relatively stable partnerships. Waiting until a relationship reaches a breaking point may limit the effectiveness of therapy, as entrenched patterns of behavior can become more challenging to shift over time.

Individuals can approach the process with a more open mind and realistic expectations by debunking these myths surrounding couples therapy. Understanding that therapy is a continuous journey toward growth and connection allows couples to invest wholeheartedly in the process without being discouraged by immediate results or misconceptions about when to seek help.

Embracing Realistic Expectations in Couples Therapy

In couples therapy, it is vital to establish realistic expectations and acknowledge the commitment required for lasting change. Therapy is not a quick fix but a process that demands sustained effort and dedication from both partners. It is essential to understand that progress may not always be linear, and setbacks are a natural part of the journey toward healthier relationship dynamics. Patience and persistence are key virtues to cultivate throughout the therapeutic process.

Setting realistic expectations is crucial in navigating the complexities of couples therapy. Rather than anticipating immediate results, it is important to recognize that meaningful change takes time to manifest. By approaching therapy with an open mind and a willingness to engage in introspection, individuals can lay a solid foundation for growth and transformation within their relationship. Consistent effort and a proactive attitude drive positive outcomes in therapy sessions.

Embracing the reality that therapy is a long-term investment in the relationship can alleviate pressure and foster a sense of hope and optimism. Couples who embark on this journey together must be prepared to confront challenges, explore vulnerabilities, and communicate openly with each other. Through this shared commitment to growth, couples can deepen their understanding of one another and develop effective strategies for resolving conflicts constructively.

Partners need to approach therapy with a willingness to learn and grow individually and as a couple. This requires a degree of vulnerability, humility, and openness to receiving feedback and guidance from a trained therapist. By embracing the process with courage and openness, couples can create a safe space for exploration, reflection, and healing within the therapeutic setting.

Therapy is a platform for couples to address underlying issues, improve communication skills, and strengthen emotional bonds. By recognizing the necessity for sustained effort and realistic expectations in therapy, partners can cultivate resilience, empathy, and understanding within their relationship. Through consistent engagement with therapeutic techniques and strategies, couples can pave the way for profound transformation and lasting intimacy in their partnership.

Therapy is not just a reactive measure for couples facing severe relationship issues; it is also a proactive tool for maintaining and enhancing healthy connections. By recognizing therapy as a useful tool for both preventive care and resolving deep-seated issues, couples can cultivate a stronger foundation for their relationship. Engaging in therapy when the relationship is already in distress is common, but waiting until problems escalate can make the process more challenging. Taking a proactive approach by seeking therapy before significant issues arise can help couples build essential skills and address minor concerns before they become major obstacles.

Preventive therapy can be likened to routine maintenance for a car; it may not seem necessary at the moment, but consistent check-ups and tune-ups can prevent breakdowns down the road. Similarly, regular therapy sessions can help couples identify and address potential areas of conflict before they escalate into serious problems. It serves as a space for open communication, reflection, and growth, fostering a deeper understanding between partners.

On the other hand, therapy can also be a powerful tool for addressing deeply rooted issues that have been causing distress in the relationship over time. By delving into these underlying concerns with the guidance of a therapist, couples can work towards healing past wounds and changing harmful patterns of behavior. It offers a safe environment for exploring vulnerabilities, expressing emotions, and rebuilding trust.

Therapy provides couples valuable tools and strategies to navigate challenges effectively, whether tackling long-standing issues or proactively strengthening their bond. By recognizing therapy as a multifaceted resource that can benefit relationships in various stages, couples can approach it with an open mind and a willingness to engage fully in the process.

In essence, whether seeking therapy to resolve existing conflicts or prevent future ones, couples stand to gain valuable insights and skills that can transform their relationship dynamics positively. By embracing therapy as an opportunity for growth, healing, and connection, partners can embark on a more fulfilling and harmonious partnership.

Debunking myths about couples therapy is not just about correcting false beliefs; it's about setting the stage for meaningful and lasting change in your relationship. The idea that therapy offers instant solutions or is only for moments of severe crisis is misleading. Recognizing this allows us to approach therapy with realistic expectations, understanding that it is a progressive journey requiring sustained effort and commitment.

You should now have a clearer perspective on how couples therapy truly functions. It's a tool designed not only to mend but also to maintain and enhance the quality of your relationship. Embracing therapy as a preventive measure can help you and your partner stay connected and address issues before they escalate.

The benefits of this realistic approach are extensive. It fosters a deeper understanding between partners, encourages consistent personal growth, and builds resilience within the relationship. As we progress in this book, you'll discover practical strategies and actionable advice to empower you to control your relationship's health.

Remember, every step you take in therapy is a step towards a more fulfilling partnership. You can transform challenges into opportunities for growth and deeper connections. Let's continue this journey together, embracing each tool and technique with openness and dedication. The path ahead is promising, and the skills you develop will rejuvenate your relationship and enrich your interaction with your loved one.

Chapter 2: Daily Doses of Connection: Integrating Therapy into Routine

"The best thing to hold onto in life is each other."

Audrey Hepburn

Transform Your Relationship One Day at a Time

The journey to a healthier, more vibrant relationship might not always require grand gestures or intense therapy sessions. Sometimes, the secret lies in the small, consistent practices integrated into your daily life. This chapter delves into how couples can enhance their connection by embedding therapeutic techniques into everyday interactions. The idea is simple yet profound: therapy doesn't end at the counselor's office; it is a continuous process that thrives on regularity and dedication.

Embedding Therapeutic Techniques

Imagine turning mundane daily interactions into opportunities to strengthen your relationship. By learning to apply therapeutic techniques in regular conversations, you can transform typical exchanges into moments of deep connection and understanding. This approach not only makes therapy more accessible but also less daunting, as it becomes part of your routine rather than an occasional intervention.

Cultivating Positive Habits

Gratitude and quick resolution of misunderstandings are like the oil that keeps the engine of your relationship running smoothly. Making these actions habitual ensures that small grievances don't turn into lasting resentments and that appreciation becomes a cornerstone of daily interactions. These habits are powerful tools that can significantly improve the quality of your relationship.

Consistency Leads to Lasting Change

Recognizing that lasting change in relationship dynamics comes from consistency is important. Regularly applying learned behaviors and communication strategies from therapy sessions helps solidify these changes, making improvements more durable and less susceptible to backsliding. This chapter emphasizes how consistent behavioral changes are crucial for truly transformative results in any relationship.

Therapy is often perceived as a remedy for times of crisis, but its true power lies in preventing those crises from occurring in the first place. By integrating therapeutic practices into your daily life, you address issues as they arise and build a stronger foundation, preventing many potential problems from ever surfacing. This proactive approach to relationship maintenance is both effective and empowering.

Implementing these strategies does not require massive shifts in your daily routine; it involves small, manageable adjustments that collectively lead to significant improvements. The beauty of this approach lies in its simplicity and the fact that it empowers couples to take control of their relational health on a day-to-day basis.

This chapter will explore practical ways to make therapy an integral part of your life without overwhelming you or your partner. You'll discover how easy it is to start small with these techniques and gradually build a robust framework for a healthy, thriving relationship. By the end of this discussion, you will be equipped with the knowledge and tools necessary to seamlessly incorporate therapeutic insights into your everyday interactions—a true game changer in relationship enhancement.

Incorporating therapeutic techniques into daily interactions is a powerful way to enhance your relationship. It's not just about the formal therapy sessions; it's about weaving these practices into your everyday life. Integrating small actions like active listening, expressing gratitude, or resolving conflicts promptly can strengthen the bond with your partner and foster a healthier dynamic. These daily doses of connection are the building blocks for long-term relationship success.

One key strategy is to practice active listening. This involves fully concentrating on what your partner is saying without interrupting, judging, or formulating a response while they speak. You show respect and empathy by truly understanding their perspective and feelings, laying the foundation for effective communication and connection. Regularly engaging in active listening can prevent misunderstandings and promote a deeper understanding of each other.

Expressing gratitude is another vital component in integrating therapy techniques into your routine. Taking time each day to acknowledge and appreciate your partner's positive traits, actions, or gestures can foster a sense of closeness and mutual appreciation. Simple acts of gratitude, whether verbal affirmations or small gestures of kindness, can go a long way in reinforcing your emotional bond and creating a positive atmosphere in your relationship.

Resolving conflicts promptly is essential for maintaining a healthy relationship. Instead of letting disagreements fester or escalate into larger issues, address them openly and honestly as they arise. Effective conflict resolution involves active listening, expressing emotions constructively, finding common ground, and seeking solutions together. By tackling challenges head-on and working through disagreements respectfully, you can prevent resentment from building up and cultivate a more harmonious partnership.

Integrating Therapy Techniques into Daily Interactions

Incorporating simple yet powerful habits into your daily routine can significantly impact the health of your relationship. Showing gratitude and resolving misunderstandings promptly are two essential practices that can cultivate a strong foundation of connection and understanding with your partner. When you express gratitude, you acknowledge and appreciate the efforts and qualities of your partner, fostering a positive atmosphere of love and support in your relationship. Similarly, addressing misunderstandings swiftly prevents small issues from escalating into larger conflicts, maintaining harmony and clarity between you and your partner.

Gratitude serves as a potent antidote to negativity and resentment in relationships. Regularly expressing appreciation for your partner's actions, qualities, or presence reinforces a sense of value and acknowledgment within the relationship. These expressions of gratitude can be as simple as saying "thank you" for a small gesture or writing a heartfelt note to show your appreciation. By making gratitude a customary practice, you create a culture of positivity that uplifts both partners and strengthens the emotional bond between you.

When it comes to resolving misunderstandings promptly,

timeliness is key. Instead of letting disagreements linger and fester, address them immediately to prevent further tension. Effective communication plays a crucial role here; ensure that both partners can express their thoughts and feelings openly and honestly. Active listening, empathy, and a willingness to understand each other's perspectives are vital components of resolving misunderstandings constructively.

Integrating these habits into daily interactions lays the groundwork for a relationship built on mutual respect, understanding, and appreciation. Consistency is key in maintaining these practices over time, as they contribute to your partnership's overall well-being and vitality. Remember that small gestures of gratitude and prompt resolution of misunderstandings can significantly impact the quality of your relationship, nurturing connection and intimacy between you and your partner.

As you cultivate these habits with your partner, observe how they positively influence the dynamics of your relationship. Notice the shifts in communication patterns, emotional closeness, and conflict resolution strategies as you express gratitude and promptly address misunderstandings. Embrace these changes as opportunities for growth and connection within your relationship, knowing that even small daily actions can lead to profound transformations in how you relate to each other.

In summary, incorporating gratitude expressions and timely resolution of misunderstandings into your daily routine creates a nurturing environment where love, understanding, and connection thrive. These simple yet impactful practices pave the way for deeper intimacy, effective communication, and lasting harmony in your relationship. Stay committed to cultivating these habits consistently, knowing they can revitalize and strengthen your bond with your partner.

In relationships, consistent behavioral changes are crucial in fostering improvement and growth. It's not just about occasional grand gestures or momentary efforts; it's the daily, consistent actions that make a difference. These small, intentional changes in behavior can lead to significant shifts in relationship dynamics over time. By recognizing the importance of consistency, couples can create a solid foundation for long-lasting positive changes in their connection.

Consistency is the key to sustainable progress in relationships. It involves implementing therapeutic techniques and strategies daily, even when challenges arise. Consistent behavioral changes require dedication and effort but yield profound results in strengthening the bond between partners. By consciously prioritizing these changes regularly, couples can create a positive ripple effect that permeates all aspects of their relationship.

One of the fundamental aspects of consistent behavioral changes is the willingness to adapt and evolve together. Relationships are dynamic entities that require ongoing adjustments and fine-tuning. By remaining open to feedback, actively listening to each other's needs, and adapting behaviors accordingly, couples can navigate challenges more effectively and grow stronger together. This flexibility and willingness to change significantly build a resilient and thriving relationship.

Couples need to stay committed to their shared goals and

aspirations. Consistency in behavior stems from a deep dedication to the relationship and a mutual desire for growth and connection. By aligning their actions with their intentions, couples can bridge the gap between where they are now and where they want to be in their relationship journey. This commitment is a guiding force propels them forward, even during challenging times.

Incorporating consistent behavioral changes into daily routines requires persistence and patience. Rome wasn't built in a day; similarly, lasting relationship improvements take time to manifest. Couples can stay motivated and inspired to continue their journey toward deeper connection and intimacy by setting realistic expectations and celebrating small victories. Every small step towards positive change contributes to the overall progress in the relationship.

By recognizing the pivotal role of consistent behavioral changes, couples can empower themselves to take charge of their relationship destiny. It's not about waiting for external circumstances to change; it's about proactively shaping the future they envision together through intentional actions each day. This proactive approach fosters a sense of empowerment and control over one's relationship path, instilling confidence and resilience in facing whatever challenges may come their way.

In summary, embracing consistent behavioral changes as a cornerstone of relationship enhancement sets the stage for transformative growth and lasting intimacy. Couples can cultivate a strong foundation built on trust, communication, and mutual respect through daily commitment, adaptability, and unwavering dedication. The journey towards a more fulfilling relationship begins with these small yet impactful steps taken consistently daily.

In a world where daily interactions shape the core of our relationships, it becomes imperative to weave therapeutic practices into these moments to foster lasting connection and understanding. This chapter has underscored the vital role of integrating therapy techniques into routine interactions to rejuvenate and sustain relationship health. Such integration enhances communication and deepens intimacy through continuous, everyday efforts rather than relying solely on sporadic therapy sessions.

Step-by-Step Process: "Seamless Integration for Relationship Revival"

The goal of this structured approach is to make therapeutic practices a natural part of your daily interaction with your partner, ensuring that every day contributes to the health and growth of your relationship. Here's how you can implement this:

1. **Identify and Understand:** Select therapeutic techniques that resonate with your relationship goals. Techniques like active listening, empathy exercises, and gratitude sharing are foundational. Dedicate time to fully understand these practices and how they can be adapted to your daily routines.

2. **Set Specific Goals:** Establish clear, achievable goals such

as incorporating active listening into your dinner conversations or expressing gratitude every morning. This specificity will guide your efforts and provide a benchmark for success.

3. **Create Reminders:** Utilize tools like alarms or sticky notes to remind you of your commitment throughout the day. These small prompts will help keep you focused and motivated.

4. **Practice and Reflect:** Consistently apply these techniques in everyday interactions and reflect on their impact. Notice any shifts in your communication patterns and overall relationship dynamics.

5. **Adjust and Celebrate:** Be open to adjusting based on what is or isn't working. Celebrate the progress, no matter how small, recognizing that each step forward is a building block in strengthening your bond.

6. **Cultivate Gratitude and Resolve Conflicts:** Make gratitude a daily practice and address misunderstandings promptly. This proactive approach prevents small issues from escalating into larger problems.

7. **Commit to Consistent Change:** Acknowledge that lasting change requires time and patience. Regularly check in with each other about these changes, offering support and encouragement as you both adapt to new behaviors.

8. **Evaluate and Adapt:** Keep track of your progress and be prepared to make changes as your relationship evolves. This ongoing evaluation will help you stay aligned with each other's needs and relationship goals.

By embracing these steps, you apply what is learned in therapy and create a resilient foundation for your relationship, characterized by mutual understanding, respect, and love. The commitment to integrating therapeutic techniques into daily routines is a testament to the dedication to maintaining and actively improving your partnership.

Let this chapter catalyze you and your partner to begin a transformative journey toward a healthier, more connected relationship. By taking these small, consistent steps, you are setting the stage for a dynamic where growth and intimacy go hand in hand, paving the way for a fulfilling partnership that stands the test of time.

Chapter 3: Spark Alive: Rituals to Reconnect

"True love stories never have endings."

Richard Bach

Is Your Relationship Losing Its Spark? Reignite It with Proven Strategies

Maintaining a vibrant and fulfilling relationship often feels like navigating an intricate dance. As time progresses, the initial spark that once defined the connection can diminish, leaving couples distant or disconnected. However, it's crucial to recognize that this is a common phase in many long-term relationships. The key to overcoming this challenge is intentional acts of connection—rituals, and routines that ensure both partners feel valued and connected.

Scheduled intimacy and connection rituals are at the heart of strengthening any romantic partnership. These are not just calendar entries but powerful tools for sustaining and enhancing the bond between partners. Regularly scheduled activities such as date nights, weekend getaways, or even nightly discussions can serve as vital touchpoints that keep the relationship dynamic and engaging.

Why Scheduled Intimacy Matters

Scheduled intimacy might sound clinical at first, but it is fundamentally about creating a space where both partners can reconnect without the distractions of daily life. It's about prioritizing your relationship and affirming that it's as crucial as any other appointment in your busy schedule. By setting aside dedicated time for one another, you signal each other that the relationship is a priority worth nurturing.

Design Connection Rituals That Work for You

Each couple is unique, so there's no one-size-fits-all approach to choosing your rituals. It could be as simple as having coffee together every morning or as elaborate as a monthly day exploring new places. The essence is to find activities both partners can look forward to—ones that resonate with your shared interests and relationship goals.

Preventing Disconnect Before It Starts

The proactive approach of establishing connection rituals also plays a crucial role in preventing feelings of neglect or emotional drift. Consistent engagement helps mitigate misunderstandings and builds a strong foundation of mutual respect and affection. Moreover, these rituals offer regular opportunities for couples to check in on each other's needs and desires, adapting to changes in their relationship landscape with agility and empathy.

This chapter will explore these strategies more deeply, equipping you with practical tools to apply in your relationship. By understanding the importance of these rituals, designing activities tailored to your unique bond, and recognizing their role in preventing disconnect, you will be well on your way to rekindling and maintaining the spark that brought you together.

Remember, keeping the spark alive is not about grand gestures; rather, it's about the cumulative effect of regular, small acts of love and attention—acts that say "you matter" day after day. Embrace these strategies with an open heart and watch them transform your relationship from routine to remarkable.

In relationships, maintaining intimacy and connection requires intentional effort. Scheduled intimacy and routine connection rituals are crucial in nurturing the bond between partners. Over time, the initial spark that brought two people together can dim, leading to feelings of disconnect or neglect. Incorporating regular activities like date nights or partner check-ins into your relationship can reignite the flame and strengthen your emotional and physical closeness.

These rituals serve as anchors in the relationship, grounding both partners in their commitment. Consistent acts of intentional connection help build a sense of security and trust, which is essential for a healthy partnership. Whether setting aside time each week for a shared activity or dedicating a few minutes daily to check in, these practices reinforce the foundation of your relationship.

In the hustle and bustle of daily life, it's easy to let quality time with your partner slip through the cracks. Creating a routine around connection ensures you prioritize each other amidst work, family obligations, and other responsibilities. These moments become sacred, exclusively for nurturing your relationship and deepening your bond.

By establishing regular rituals of connection, you are investing in your present and safeguarding your future together. Preventing feelings of neglect or disconnect before they escalate is key to maintaining a strong and vibrant relationship. Consistency in these practices lays the groundwork for open communication, trust, and mutual understanding.

Embracing Consistent Intimacy and Meaningful Check-Ins

Regular activities such as date nights and partner check-ins are essential in nurturing and strengthening the bond between couples. Designing these routines can inject excitement and anticipation into the relationship, fostering a deeper connection and understanding between partners. Date nights allow couples to step away from the demands of daily life and focus solely on each other, rekindling romance and intimacy in a dedicated setting. By setting aside time for these special occasions, partners can prioritize their relationship and show appreciation for one another's presence.

Partner check-ins serve as a valuable tool for communication, enabling couples to openly discuss their feelings, concerns, and desires in a safe space. These regular conversations allow partners to express their needs, listen actively, and address any issues that may arise. By engaging in consistent dialogue, couples can build trust, strengthen emotional bonds, and cultivate a sense of unity within the relationship. Regular communication fosters understanding and empathy, laying the foundation for a supportive and harmonious partnership.

When designing these activities, it is crucial to tailor them to suit the unique dynamics of the relationship. Couples should consider each other's preferences, interests, and schedules to ensure these rituals are enjoyable and sustainable. Variety is key in keeping these routines fresh and engaging, so exploring different date night ideas or adjusting the format of partner check-ins can prevent monotony and spark creativity within the relationship.

Consistency is paramount in maintaining the effectiveness of these rituals. By committing to regular date nights and partner check-ins, couples demonstrate dedication to nurturing their connection over time. These activities should be viewed as nonnegotiable appointments that hold significance in prioritizing the relationship amidst life's inevitable challenges and distractions.

Through intentional design and unwavering commitment, scheduled intimacy rituals can reinvigorate relationships, deepen emotional bonds, and foster long-lasting connections between partners. By investing time and effort into these shared experiences, couples can create lasting memories, cultivate mutual respect, and fortify their partnership against potential strains or conflicts. Ultimately, these activities are a beacon of light, guiding couples toward sustained closeness, understanding, and love.

Consistent, intentional acts prevent feelings of disconnect and neglect within a relationship. By engaging in regular, deliberate efforts to connect with your partner, you actively reinforce the emotional bond that sustains your partnership. These intentional acts are a powerful reminder of your commitment to each other, creating a sense of security and closeness that can weather any storm. Small gestures of love and appreciation can go a long way in nurturing the connection between you and your partner.

One key aspect of preventing feelings of neglect is active listening. When you truly listen to your partner without judgment or distraction, you show them their thoughts and feelings are valued. This act of attentive listening fosters understanding and empathy, strengthening the emotional foundation of your relationship. Regular communication that involves both speaking and listening ensures that both partners feel heard and understood.

Another vital component in preventing disconnect is shared experiences. You create lasting memories that strengthen your bond by engaging in activities, whether cooking a meal, walking, or pursuing a hobby. Shared experiences build a sense of unity and partnership, reinforcing that you are on this journey together. These moments of togetherness help rekindle the spark in your relationship, reminding you both why you fell in love in the first place.

Consistency is key when it comes to preventing feelings of neglect. Making intentional acts a routine ensures that your relationship remains a priority. Setting aside dedicated time for each other helps maintain the emotional connection essential for a healthy partnership. Consistent acts of love and kindness build trust and intimacy, creating a solid foundation for your relationship to thrive.

Incorporating rituals into your daily life can also prevent feelings of disconnect and neglect. Whether it's a morning coffee together, an evening walk, or a weekly movie night, these rituals provide stability and predictability in your relationship. Rituals create a sense of security and comfort, reinforcing the idea that you can count on each other no matter what challenges may arise. These shared rituals strengthen the bond between you and your partner, fostering a deep connection.

By understanding how consistent intentional acts can prevent feelings of disconnect and neglect, you empower yourself to take proactive steps in nurturing your relationship. You can ensure your partnership remains strong and vibrant through active listening, shared experiences, consistency, and rituals. These intentional acts serve as the building blocks of a healthy, thriving relationship, fostering love, trust, and intimacy between you and your partner.

Maintaining the vibrancy of a relationship requires more than love and good intentions. It demands consistent, deliberate actions that reinforce the bond between partners. Couples can cultivate emotional and physical closeness through scheduled intimacy and connection routines, ensuring the spark remains alive.

Scheduled intimacy is not about rigidly timing moments of connection but prioritizing each other regularly. By setting aside specific times for deep, meaningful interactions, couples can avoid the common pitfall of letting their busy lives drift them apart. This could be as simple as a weekly date night or a daily few minutes of uninterrupted conversation. The key is consistency; these rituals become the heartbeat of the relationship, keeping the connection strong and resilient.

Regular activities such as date nights or partner check-ins serve a dual purpose. They provide opportunities for enjoyment and relaxation and create a safe space for sharing feelings and concerns. This ongoing dialogue is crucial for understanding each other's evolving needs and expectations. It's about staying updated with each other's lives and growing together rather than apart.

Preventing feelings of disconnect and neglect is perhaps one of the most critical aspects of these rituals. Consistent, intentional acts of connection buffer against life's challenges for every couple. They build a foundation of trust and mutual respect, which can make all the difference when navigating difficult times. By maintaining these practices, couples can address potential issues proactively rather than letting them fester into bigger problems.

It's important to remember that every couple is unique, and so should their rituals of connection. What works for one couple might not work for another. Therefore, it's beneficial to experiment with different activities and schedules to find what best helps you reconnect and rekindle your relationship.

Take action today by setting up your first scheduled connection—plan a date, a quiet coffee together, or simply a time to talk undisturbed. Make this practice a cornerstone of your relationship, and watch as it transforms your connection, deepening the intimacy and strength between you both. Remember, the health of your relationship greatly depends on your willingness to invest time and effort into maintaining its warmth and closeness. Embrace these simple yet powerful rituals, and ensure your partnership survives and thrives.

Chapter 4: Structured Success: Embracing EFT and the Gottman Method

"Relationships fail because people take their own

insecurities and try to twist them into

their partner's flaws."

Baylor Barbee

Transform Your Relationship: Why Structured Therapies Work

When relationships falter, it's not just the heart that feels the weight but also the profound confusion about where things went wrong and how to fix them. This is where embracing structured therapeutic methods like Emotional Focused Therapy (EFT) and the Gottman Method can be transformative. These approaches are not just about fixing what's broken; they're about understanding the deep emotional undercurrents and learning new ways to connect and communicate effectively.

EFT and the Gottman Method stand out in the landscape of couples therapy due to their robust, research-backed frameworks. They offer more than temporary fixes; they provide a roadmap for deep, lasting relationship change. Focusing on emotional engagement and practical communication skills, these therapies help couples move from distress to recovery, eventually to a stronger, more resilient connection.

The Power of EFT

Emotional Focused Therapy revolves around the science of attachment, emphasizing emotional bonding and responsiveness between partners. The foundational concept here is straightforward: emotional responses shape our relationships. EFT helps couples understand how their emotional reactions can create patterns that strengthen or weaken their bonds. Through structured stages, EFT guides couples in reshaping these interactions into healthier, more supportive behaviors that foster security and trust.

The Clarity of the Gottman Method

On the other hand, **the Gottman Method** provides practical strategies based on decades of observational research. It identifies specific behaviors that predict relationship success and failure, famously through Dr. John Gottman's 'Four Horsemen of the Apocalypse' model, which outlines communication styles that can predict the end of a relationship. By teaching couples to recognize and resolve conflicts through healthy communication techniques, this method addresses problems as they arise and helps prevent them.

Both therapies underscore the importance of addressing issues as they come and building a foundation strong enough to handle future challenges. They equip couples with tools to heal and thrive by enhancing understanding, empathy, and connection.

Harnessing Structured Approaches for Deeper Connection

By applying interventions from both EFT and the Gottman Method, couples can expect significant improvements in communicating during conflicts and connecting emotionally during peaceful times. These interventions are designed to be direct and impactful, ensuring that each step is towards a deeper bond.

Achieving deeper emotional connections is at the heart of these therapies. They are structured specifically to break through surface-level interactions and delve into deeper emotional realms, which often go unexplored but are crucial for lasting intimacy. This process is not just about learning techniques but about transforming an understanding of oneself and one's partner at a fundamental level.

The journey through EFT and the Gottman Method isn't just about navigating rough waters and setting sail towards a horizon of renewed connection and understanding. By committing to these structured therapeutic approaches, couples can rediscover their relationship's potential—surviving challenges and thriving through them.

As we explore these powerful therapeutic tools further in this chapter, remember: The goal is not merely to manage relationship troubles as they occur but to build enduring strategies for emotional connectivity and mutual understanding that will sustain your partnership for years.

Emotional Focused Therapy (EFT) and the Gottman Method are powerful tools for transforming relationships due to their structured and evidence-based approaches. These methods offer concrete strategies to enhance communication, manage conflicts, and foster deeper emotional connections. Providing specific interventions backed by research, EFT and the Gottman Method offer a clear path toward creating secure and resilient relationship bonds.

In EFT, the focus is on identifying and addressing underlying emotions that drive relationship behaviors. Partners can build a stronger emotional connection by recognizing and validating these emotions. The Gottman Method, on the other hand, emphasizes improving communication patterns and conflict resolution skills through practical exercises and interventions. Both approaches complement each other by addressing different aspects of relationship dynamics.

Understanding the foundational concepts of EFT involves recognizing the importance of emotional responsiveness in relationships. This therapy method highlights how emotional attunement can create a safe space for partners to express themselves authentically. EFT aims to deepen intimacy and strengthen the bond between partners by prioritizing emotions and vulnerabilities.

The Gottman Method enhances communication skills by introducing specific tools for constructive dialogue. Partners can improve communication through active listening, expressing needs clearly, and validating emotions. Additionally, this method offers strategies for managing conflicts healthily and productively.

By combining the principles of EFT and the Gottman Method, couples can experience profound transformations in their relationships. The structured nature of these therapeutic approaches provides a roadmap for navigating challenges and fostering growth. Through consistent practice and application of these techniques, partners can cultivate a deeper understanding of each other and create a more fulfilling connection.

Applying EFT and the Gottman Method

We must implement these powerful techniques now that we have delved into the foundational concepts of Emotional Focused Therapy (EFT) and the Gottman Method. Applying specific interventions from these methods can enhance communication and resolve conflicts in your relationship. Implementing targeted strategies can pave the way for a more harmonious and fulfilling connection with your partner.

Enhancing Communication: Communication lies at the core of any successful relationship. One key aspect of EFT and the Gottman Method is their focus on improving how partners communicate. Practice active listening to truly understand your partner's perspective without immediately formulating a response. Express your thoughts and feelings openly and honestly, using "I" statements to avoid blame or accusation. By fostering a safe space for dialogue, you can strengthen the foundation of your relationship.

Resolving Conflicts: Conflicts are inevitable in any relationship, but how you navigate them can make all the difference. EFT emphasizes identifying underlying emotions driving conflicts and helping partners express their vulnerable feelings rather than resorting to defensiveness or anger. The Gottman Method introduces tools like the "Softened Startup," encouraging gentle and respectful approaches when discussing sensitive topics. By acknowledging each other's perspectives and working towards mutually beneficial solutions, conflicts can transform into opportunities for growth.

Implementing Rituals of Connection: Both EFT and the Gottman Method advocate for establishing rituals of connection in your daily lives. These rituals could be as simple as sharing a morning coffee or taking an evening walk hand in hand. Such practices help deepen emotional bonds by creating moments of intimacy and shared experiences. By prioritizing these rituals, you reinforce the emotional connection between you and your partner.

Building Trust: Trust forms the bedrock of a healthy relationship. You can gradually rebuild or strengthen trust with your partner by consistently applying EFT and Gottman interventions. Honor commitments and follow through on promises, demonstrating reliability and dependability. Validate your partner's emotions even when you may not agree with their perspective, showing empathy and understanding in challenging situations.

Celebrating Successes: As you embark on this journey to revitalize your relationship through EFT and the Gottman Method, remember to celebrate small victories. Acknowledge moments where communication was particularly effective, or conflicts were resolved amicably. Recognizing these successes reinforces positive patterns and motivates continued growth within your relationship.

Incorporating these specific interventions into your daily interactions with your partner can yield significant improvements in communication, conflict resolution, emotional connection, and overall relationship satisfaction. Stay committed to practicing these techniques consistently, and witness the transformation of your relationship into a more resilient and fulfilling bond.

Framework: Relationship Enhancement Model

A Relationship Enhancement Model is proposed to effectively integrate Emotional Focused Therapy (EFT) and the Gottman Method into couples' dynamics. This model aims to guide couples through the challenges commonly encountered in therapy, offering a structured approach to achieving deeper emotional connections. By outlining the fundamental concepts of both therapeutic methods and providing practical interventions, this model equips couples with the tools to navigate emotional responses to resistance and ultimately enhance their relationship dynamics.

Understanding Fundamentals

The first step in the Relationship Enhancement Model involves familiarizing couples with the foundational principles of EFT and the Gottman Method. This initial phase sets the groundwork for understanding each approach's purpose, processes, and expected outcomes. By gaining insight into how these methods operate and their specific goals for relationship improvement, couples can establish a solid foundation for their therapeutic journey.

Implementing Interventions

Following an understanding of the fundamentals, the model then focuses on implementing specific interventions unique to each method. The "Dance of Connection" facilitates emotional bonding and secure attachment for EFT. On the other hand, the Gottman Method's "Four Horsemen of the Apocalypse" helps identify destructive communication patterns that must be addressed. By incorporating these interventions into their interactions, couples can address underlying issues and improve their communication styles effectively.

Navigating Emotional Responses

In any therapeutic process, emotional responses and resistance are common challenges that couples may encounter. This phase of the model provides strategies for navigating these emotional reactions, ensuring that couples can stay focused on their therapeutic goals despite potential setbacks. By acknowledging and addressing emotional barriers, couples can work towards building stronger emotional connections and fostering healthier relationship dynamics.

Phased Integration Approach

The final part of the Relationship Enhancement Model outlines a phased integration approach for couples to incorporate EFT and the Gottman Method into their interactions gradually. By setting weekly goals and engaging in reflective practices, couples can track their progress and steadily improve their relationship dynamics. This structured approach encourages consistency and commitment to the therapeutic process, leading to long-lasting positive changes in how couples relate to each other.

Visual Aids

To enhance understanding and facilitate implementation, visual aids such as flowcharts, diagrams illustrating communication patterns targeted by each method, and comparison tables are included in the model. These visual representations help couples identify their current relationship states versus therapy objectives, making it easier to track progress and adjust strategies as needed. The visual aids are valuable tools for promoting active engagement with the therapeutic process.

In summary, the Relationship Enhancement Model provides a structured framework for couples to deepen their emotional connections through integrating EFT and the Gottman Method into their relationship dynamics. Following this model's guidance, couples can navigate challenges effectively, implement targeted interventions, and achieve lasting improvements in communication and emotional intimacy.

Pathways to Partnership: A Step-by-Step Guide to Revitalizing Your Relationship

Emotional-focused therapy (EFT) and the Gottman Method have effectively transformed relationships through structured, research-backed strategies. By understanding these methods deeply, applying their specific interventions, and committing to ongoing structured therapeutic approaches, couples can expect significant improvements in communication, conflict resolution, and emotional intimacy.

Step 1: Understanding the Foundational Concepts of EFT and the Gottman Method

Begin your journey by immersing yourself in the core principles of EFT and the Gottman Method. Gather information from reliable sources and distill the crucial elements into a digestible format to refer back to throughout your relationship enhancement process. Engage your partner in discussions about these insights, setting clear goals for what you hope to achieve together. If possible, seek support from a professional therapist trained in these methods to guide you with precision.

Step 2: Applying Specific Interventions to Enhance Communication and Resolve Conflicts

With a solid understanding of the methods, start integrating targeted interventions into your daily interactions. Practice vulnerability in expressing emotions with EFT techniques or adopt the Gottman Method's softened startup approach to address sensitive issues. Regularly evaluate the impact of these interventions on your relationship, adjusting as necessary to better fit your unique dynamic.

Step 3: Achieving Deeper Emotional Connections Through Structured Therapeutic Approaches

Deepen your emotional connection by consistently applying structured therapeutic strategies. Set aside time for regular therapy sessions, engage in couple's exercises that foster intimacy, and utilize recommended resources like workbooks or therapeutic assignments. Commitment to these practices may be challenging, but the rewards of a revitalized relationship are well worth the effort.

By following these steps, you enhance your partnership and empower yourselves with tools that foster a resilient, loving connection. Embrace these structured approaches with an open heart and a committed spirit, and watch as your relationship transforms into a source of profound joy and fulfillment.

Chapter 5: Serenity Together: Mindfulness and Stress Management

"A successful relationship requires falling in love

multiple times, but always with

the same person."

Mignon McLaughlin

From Tension to Tranquility: Unlocking Peace in Partnership

In the bustling rhythm of daily life, stress often becomes a silent saboteur in relationships, creeping in and clouding communication, empathy, and connection. Recognizing this, mindfulness emerges as a personal practice and a crucial tool for couples striving to deepen their bond and navigate the complexities of modern life together. The essence of mindfulness—being present in the moment without judgment—can transform interactions between partners, allowing for more thoughtful communication and a greater understanding of each other's emotional landscapes.

Stress management is equally vital. It's about more than just avoiding arguments or managing hectic schedules; it involves developing strategies that foster resilience and stability within the relationship. When both partners commit to managing their stress effectively, they protect their emotional bandwidth and keep their relationship from becoming another source of strain. This dual approach—mindfulness and proactive stress management—forms a robust framework for sustaining and enriching romantic partnerships.

Embracing Mindfulness: A Pathway to Connection

Implementing mindfulness practices such as meditation or yoga offers profound benefits for relationships. These practices help individuals cultivate calm awareness, which can dramatically improve how they interact with their partner. By fostering mindfulness, couples can achieve a deeper connection and more meaningful interactions, effectively enhancing the overall quality of their relationship.

The Ripple Effects of Stress Management

Understanding how managing stress impacts communication underscores its importance in maintaining harmony within a relationship. Stress often triggers defensive or aggressive communication styles, escalating conflicts rather than resolving them. Learning effective stress management techniques allows individuals to approach discussions with composure, reducing misunderstandings and promoting healthier interactions.

Building Emotional Resilience Together

Lastly, fostering emotional resilience is pivotal in navigating the ups and downs of any relationship. Resilient couples can face challenges without losing their sense of perspective or emotional connection. This resilience supports individual well-being and fortifies the relationship against external pressures that could cause discord.

This chapter will explore these three key areas—mindfulness practices, effective stress management, and the cultivation of emotional resilience—to guide couples on their journey toward a more peaceful and fulfilling partnership. By integrating these practices into daily life, couples can enhance their ability to communicate effectively, reduce conflict, and strengthen their emotional connection.

The strategies discussed here are practical and accessible, designed to fit into everyday life without overwhelming either partner. Each section provides actionable steps that couples can take to start seeing improvements in their interactions and overall relationship health immediately.

As we delve into these transformative practices, remember that the journey toward improved relational dynamics is ongoing. Each step taken is an investment in the future of your relationship—a commitment to cultivating a partnership characterized not only by love but by mutual respect, understanding, and, above all, serenity together.

In the hustle and bustle of daily life, it's easy to overlook the importance of mindfulness practices in nurturing a healthy relationship. Implementing simple yet powerful techniques like meditation or yoga can profoundly improve relational dynamics. Incorporating mindfulness into your routine can enhance emotional awareness, reduce stress, and foster a deeper connection with your partner.

Mindfulness is not just about being present in the moment; it's also about being present with your partner. When both individuals in a relationship practice mindfulness, they create a space for understanding and empathy to flourish. This heightened awareness allows for better communication, increased emotional intelligence, and a more harmonious bond overall.

Meditation can be a transformative tool for couples, allowing them to regulate emotions and respond thoughtfully rather than impulsively in challenging situations. By cultivating a regular meditation practice together, partners can develop a shared language of emotional regulation and support each other during stress or conflict.

Yoga, focusing on breathwork and physical movement, offers another avenue for couples to connect mindfully. Practicing yoga together strengthens the body and deepens the emotional connection between partners. Couples can cultivate a sense of unity and harmony that extends beyond the mat through synchronized movements and shared energy.

Incorporating these mindfulness practices into your daily routine can pave the way for a more fulfilling and balanced relationship. By taking the time to nurture your well-being through meditation or yoga, you are also investing in the health of your partnership. Cultivating mindfulness creates a solid foundation for mutual respect, understanding, and support.

Managing Stress to Improve Communication and Conflict Resolution in Relationships

Stress can be a significant barrier to effective communication and often escalates relationship conflicts. When individuals are overwhelmed by stress, they may struggle to express themselves clearly or listen attentively to their partners. This lack of communication can lead to misunderstandings and resentment and further strain the relationship. By managing stress effectively, couples can create a more conducive environment for open and honest communication.

Reducing stress levels can also help individuals regulate their emotions better, allowing them to respond to their partners with greater empathy and understanding. When stress is high, emotions can easily spiral out of control, leading to heated arguments and hurtful exchanges. By managing stress, couples can approach conversations with a calmer mindset, fostering more productive dialogues and minimizing the likelihood of escalating conflicts.

One of the key benefits of stress management in relationships is improving conflict resolution skills. When less stressed, individuals are better equipped to approach disagreements constructively and find mutually beneficial solutions. By addressing stress proactively, couples can navigate conflicts with a clearer perspective, focusing on resolving issues rather than getting caught up in negative emotions.

Effective stress management also enhances overall relationship quality by fostering a sense of mutual support. When partners prioritize stress reduction, they create a foundation of understanding and empathy that strengthens their bond. By supporting each other in managing stress, couples demonstrate care and concern for one another's well-being, building a deeper connection based on shared experiences and challenges.

Furthermore, reducing stress levels can lead to increased patience and tolerance within the relationship. When less stressed, individuals are more likely to approach disagreements with composure and patience rather than reacting impulsively. This increased emotional resilience allows couples to weather challenges more effectively, maintaining harmony even in adversity.

In summary, managing stress positively impacts communication by creating a conducive environment for open dialogue and reducing conflicts through enhanced emotional regulation and conflict resolution skills. By prioritizing stress management as a couple, individuals can nurture a supportive and understanding relationship characterized by patience, empathy, and effective communication.

Framework: Mindful Relational Dynamics Model

The **Mindful Relational Dynamics Model** is structured to guide couples in integrating mindfulness practices and stress management techniques into their daily lives to enhance their relationship. This model has several interconnected components that foster emotional resilience and perspective in relationship interactions.

Stress Triggers Identification

The initial phase of the model involves identifying stress triggers within the relationship and understanding individual reactions to these stressors. Couples are encouraged to reflect on specific situations or behaviors that increase stress. By recognizing these triggers, partners can develop awareness of potential conflict points and emotional responses.

Basic Mindfulness Exercises

Following stress trigger identification, the model introduces basic mindfulness exercises tailored to the couple's needs. These exercises may include simple breathing techniques, body scans, or guided meditations to cultivate present-moment awareness and emotional regulation. Practicing these exercises regularly can help individuals manage stress more effectively.

Routine Integration

As couples progress through the model, they are encouraged to integrate mindfulness practices into their daily routines. Suggestions such as engaging in joint meditation sessions, practicing mindful communication, or incorporating mindful walking into their schedule can help solidify these practices as habits. Consistent integration of mindfulness into daily life fosters a sense of connection and shared experiences between partners.

Advanced Conflict Management Techniques

In later phases of the model, advanced conflict management techniques are introduced, emphasizing the application of mindfulness during disagreements. Couples learn to approach conflicts with heightened empathy, reduce reactivity, and maintain perspective during challenging conversations. These advanced techniques enhance communication skills and promote a deeper understanding between partners.

Instructional Materials

The model provides instructional materials such as step-by-step guides for mindfulness exercises, tips for overcoming common pitfalls in stress management, and checklists for daily mindfulness practice adherence. These resources serve as practical tools for couples to effectively navigate the complexities of integrating mindfulness into their relationship.

The Mindful Relational Dynamics Model operates on a feedback loop system where increased awareness of stress triggers leads to improved emotional regulation and conflict management skills. By engaging with the various components of the model over time, couples can develop a strong foundation of emotional resilience and perspective in their relationship interactions.

Practically, this model offers couples a roadmap for cultivating mindfulness in their relationship, leading to enhanced communication, reduced conflict, and increased emotional connection. By following this framework and consistently practicing mindfulness techniques, partners can easily navigate challenges and deepen their bond.

As we explore the profound impact of mindfulness and stress management on relationships, it's clear that these practices are not just beneficial—they are essential. Embracing techniques such as meditation and yoga can transform the emotional dynamics between partners, fostering a deeper understanding and stronger bond. By managing stress effectively, couples can significantly improve communication, reducing conflicts and misunderstandings that often arise during tense moments.

Implementing mindfulness is more than a practice; it's a commitment to nurturing your relationship from the inside out. It equips both partners with the tools to remain present and engaged, even in challenging times. This presence is crucial as it allows for genuine interactions and a heartfelt connection that withstands the tests of everyday stresses.

The positive effects of managing stress are equally compelling. When stress is no longer a constant barrier, couples find it easier to communicate openly and without reservation. This open line of communication is vital for resolving conflicts and building a resilient partnership. Moreover, stress management helps maintain emotional balance, which is key to perceiving situations clearly and responding appropriately.

Lastly, cultivating emotional resilience through mindfulness creates a buffer against a relationship's inevitable ups and downs. It provides an invaluable perspective when navigating complex emotions and scenarios within the partnership. By fostering resilience, couples enhance their ability to cope with adversity, strengthening them individually and as a unit.

The journey towards incorporating these practices into your daily life may require patience and persistence, but the rewards are immeasurable. As you and your partner embark on this path, remember that each step forward is towards a more harmonious and fulfilling relationship. Embrace these tools with an open heart and watch your interactions' quality and connection depth improve dramatically.

Take control of your emotional and relational health by actively engaging with these mindfulness strategies. Remember, the power to change the dynamics of your relationship for the better lies in your hands. Start today and experience the transformative effects of serenity and understanding in your partnership.

Chapter 6: Therapy as a Tool: Proactive vs. Reactive Approaches

"To get the full value of joy, you must have

someone to divide it with."

Mark Twain

Is Waiting Until Things Break the Only Option?

Many couples hold the belief that therapy is a last resort, a beacon to turn to only when their relationship ship is already sinking. This chapter aims to dismantle that myth and illuminate how therapy can be a proactive toolkit for strengthening bonds before they fray. By understanding therapy as preventive care and crisis management, couples can adopt healthier approaches to nurturing their connection.

Often perceived through the lens of repair, therapy holds immense potential as a preventative measure. It's not merely about fixing what's broken but fortifying what's intact, ensuring that minor misunderstandings don't evolve into insurmountable issues. Early engagement in therapeutic practices can set a foundation for open communication, helping partners understand and appreciate each other's perspectives long before significant conflicts arise.

Misconceptions about therapy can deter couples from seeking help early when it is most effective. By only considering therapy as an option when faced with severe relationship distress, couples miss out on the benefits of using therapy as a tool for understanding and growth. This preventative approach helps smooth out small bumps in the road and avoid them altogether.

Why Wait? The Proactive Power of Therapy

Introducing therapy into your relationship doesn't signify failure; it symbolizes commitment—a commitment to mutual growth and understanding. Couples who engage in therapy before major issues arise are more likely to develop resilience against future challenges. This proactive approach fosters a deeper intimacy and connection as both partners learn effective communication skills and strategies for handling disagreements constructively.

By recognizing timely intervention as beneficial, couples can prevent problems from becoming deeply entrenched. Often, issues left unaddressed grow in complexity and intensity. Therapy offers a space to address these concerns while they are still manageable, promoting healthier interactions and reducing the likelihood of more severe conflicts in the future.

The chapter will explore strategies that encourage couples to view therapy as an emergency measure and an ongoing part of relationship maintenance. *This shift in perception* can significantly change how partners deal with potential conflicts, making their bond stronger and more resilient.

In sum, rethinking the role of therapy in relationships is crucial. It's about moving away from the crisis-driven model to one that values continuous improvement and preemptive care. By embracing therapy as a regular aspect of relationship health, couples empower themselves with tools for better understanding, communication, and problem-solving—key elements for any thriving relationship.

Therapy is often seen as a last resort, a beacon of hope when relationships are on the brink of collapse. However, this common misconception overlooks the significant benefits that therapy can offer well before reaching such dire circumstances. **It's crucial to** dispel the myth that therapy is only for relationships in crisis. Therapy can be a powerful tool for enhancing relationship health addressing minor issues before they snowball into major problems.

Many couples hesitate to seek therapy until their conflicts have escalated, fearing judgment or failure. By challenging this belief and reframing therapy as a proactive measure rather than a reactive one, couples can unlock their full potential. Therapy can serve as a preventative measure, helping couples navigate challenges early on and build a strong foundation for their relationship.

The stigma surrounding therapy often stems from misconceptions about what it entails. Instead of viewing therapy as a sign of weakness or defeat, couples can reframe it as an opportunity for growth and self-improvement. Therapy offers a safe space to explore emotions, communication patterns, and dynamics within the relationship.

Couples can develop essential skills and tools to navigate future challenges effectively by engaging in therapy before issues become insurmountable. Early intervention through therapy can equip couples with strategies to enhance communication, foster intimacy, and strengthen their bond. Rather than waiting for problems to escalate, proactive engagement with therapy empowers couples to take control of their relationship's trajectory.

Moreover, seeking therapy early on can prevent minor issues from festering and evolving into more significant concerns over time. Addressing concerns promptly can prevent them from becoming deeply entrenched within the relationship, making them more manageable and easier to resolve.

The Power of Early Engagement in Therapy for Strengthening Relationships

Engaging in therapy early on in a relationship can be a proactive step towards enhancing relationship health and strengthening the bond between partners. By seeking therapy before issues escalate, couples can address underlying concerns, improve communication skills, and develop strategies to navigate challenges effectively. Therapy is a valuable tool for nurturing a relationship, offering a safe space for both partners to express their feelings, thoughts, and concerns openly.

Encouraging early and proactive engagement with therapy can prevent minor issues from snowballing into significant problems. Taking the initiative to seek help demonstrates a commitment to the relationship and a willingness to work on its growth and development. Therapy can provide couples with insights into their dynamics, allowing them to identify areas of improvement and implement positive changes for long-term success.

Proactive engagement with therapy is not a sign of weakness but rather a demonstration of strength and dedication to the relationship. It showcases a desire to invest in the partnership and prioritize its well-being. Through therapy, couples can acquire tools to navigate conflicts constructively, deepen their emotional connection, and foster mutual understanding.

Early intervention through therapy can prevent small misunderstandings from escalating into significant barriers in communication. It equips couples with the skills to address issues as they arise, fostering a culture of open dialogue and respect within the relationship. Couples can lay a solid foundation for long-term harmony and happiness by participating in therapy sessions.

Embracing therapy as a proactive measure underscores the value of continuous growth and improvement within a relationship. It acknowledges that relationships require nurturing, attention, and sometimes outside guidance to thrive. By engaging in therapy early on, couples demonstrate their commitment to each other's well-being and shared future.

In summary, encouraging early and proactive engagement with therapy is an empowering step toward fostering a healthy and resilient relationship. It signifies a partnership's dedication to growth, improvement, and shared happiness. By recognizing the benefits of therapy as a preventative measure, couples can cultivate stronger bonds, effective communication skills, and enduring intimacy in their relationship.

Therapy can prevent deeply entrenched issues in relationships from taking root. By recognizing the signs of trouble early on and seeking help promptly, couples can address underlying issues before they escalate into significant problems. Timely intervention through therapy can offer invaluable insights and tools to navigate challenges effectively.

Communication breakdowns, unresolved conflicts, and emotional distance are warning signs that should not be ignored. These early indicators can signal potential trouble ahead if left unaddressed. Seeking therapy at this stage is not a sign of weakness but a proactive step toward nurturing a healthy relationship. Therapists can guide people in improving communication skills, fostering empathy, and resolving conflicts constructively.

Preventative therapy sessions can serve as a space for couples to strengthen their bond, enhance their understanding of each other's needs, and build a solid foundation for the future. Couples can develop healthy habits and coping mechanisms to weather challenges together by engaging in therapy before issues become deeply ingrained. Therapy is not solely reactive but can also be a proactive tool for relationship growth and resilience.

Addressing underlying dynamics that contribute to relationship strain early on can prevent these patterns from becoming entrenched. Through therapy, couples can explore the root causes of their conflicts, gain insight into their behaviors, and learn how to break negative cycles. By confronting issues head-on in a safe and supportive environment, couples can create lasting change.

Therapy offers a space for vulnerability, honesty, and growth within the relationship. It allows couples to delve into deep-seated issues, heal past wounds, and cultivate understanding and compassion for one another. By seeking timely therapy, couples demonstrate their commitment to each other's well-being and the health of their relationship.

Proactive engagement with therapy empowers couples to take charge of their relationship's trajectory and make informed choices about its future. Couples can build a strong foundation based on trust, communication, and mutual respect by acknowledging the value of preventative care in maintaining relationship health. Therapy is not just a last resort but a valuable resource for enhancing connection and intimacy in relationships.

In recognizing the significance of timely therapy in preventing deeply entrenched issues, couples pave the way for sustainable growth and transformation within their relationship. By embracing therapy as a proactive tool for nurturing connection, couples can foster resilience, deepen intimacy, and navigate challenges with newfound strength and understanding.

Therapy, often misunderstood as a last resort for troubled relationships, is, in fact, a powerful proactive tool that can significantly enhance the quality and longevity of your relationship. By engaging in therapy early, you dispense with the myth that it's only meant for relationships at the brink of collapse. This proactive approach nurtures a deeper understanding between partners and fortifies the relationship against potential future discord.

Early engagement in therapeutic practices is beneficial and a strategic move towards cultivating a robust relationship. Consider therapy as regular maintenance for your relationship, similar to how you treat your physical health. Just as you wouldn't wait for a severe illness to see a doctor, there's no need to wait for a crisis to seek therapy. This shift in perspective from reactive to proactive can transform how you and your partner relate, communicate, and understand each other.

Timely intervention through therapy can preempt the development of entrenched issues that are much harder to resolve later. It's about catching and addressing small misunderstandings before they escalate into significant conflicts. This approach doesn't just solve problems—it prevents them. By recognizing the early signs that you might benefit from professional guidance, you take control of your relationship's health, steering it towards continual growth and deeper connection.

You can change the trajectory of your relationship through informed, deliberate actions. Therapy is a tool that empowers you both to navigate the complexities of your partnership with greater clarity and empathy. Embrace it not only as a means of resolving conflict but as a way to celebrate and strengthen your bond. Take that step today—your relationship is worth it!

Chapter 7: From Conflict to Compassion: Mastering Empathy

"Love is composed of a single soul

inhabiting two bodies."

Aristotle

Is Winning the Argument Worth Losing the Connection?

When conflicts arise in relationships, it's natural to focus on who is right and who is wrong. However, this chapter delves into why understanding and empathy are far more valuable than winning arguments. Conflicts are a part of every relationship, but how we handle these disagreements can significantly affect the quality and longevity of our connections. By mastering empathy, couples can transform conflicts into opportunities for growth and deeper understanding.

Empathy involves putting yourself in your partner's shoes and truly understanding their feelings and perspectives. This chapter will explore practical techniques that enhance empathy during conflicts, helping you shift from a mindset focused on winning to one centered on understanding. Through examples and actionable advice, you'll learn how to apply these techniques in everyday situations to strengthen your relationship.

The Art of Active Listening

One critical technique we'll discuss is **active listening**. Active listening is not just about hearing your partner's words but fully engaging with them, showing genuine interest, and responding by affirming their feelings. This chapter will guide you through the steps of active listening and demonstrate how it can be a powerful tool for resolving conflicts.

Understanding Before Being Understood

Another key aspect we'll cover is the importance of seeking to understand before being understood. Often, in arguments, we're so focused on getting our point across that we don't take the time to listen to what our partner is saying. This chapter will provide strategies for reversing that habit, emphasizing the importance of validating your partner's perspective before presenting your own.

Collaborative Communication

We'll also explore how empathetic communication fosters collaboration rather than competition. When both partners feel heard and understood, they are more likely to find solutions that benefit both parties. This section will offer tips on communicating in ways that promote teamwork and mutual respect.

By the end of this chapter, you will have a toolkit of strategies for dealing with conflicts compassionately and constructively. You'll understand why empathy is crucial for resolving disputes and building a loving and resilient relationship. These tools allow you to turn every conflict into a stepping stone towards greater intimacy and understanding.

Remember, mastering empathy doesn't mean you'll never experience conflict again; it equips you with the skills to handle disagreements that strengthen your bond rather than weaken it. As you practice these techniques, you'll find that your relationship becomes more supportive, connected, and enriched—truly embodying the spirit of Love Revived.

Conflict in relationships is common, but how we approach and resolve it can make all the difference. Empathy plays a crucial role in navigating conflicts effectively. Understanding our partner's perspective and emotions can foster a deeper connection and find common ground. Techniques that enhance empathy, such as active listening and putting oneself in the other person's shoes, can transform conflicts from battlegrounds to opportunities for growth and understanding.

Active listening involves more than just hearing words; it requires full engagement with what the other person is saying. This means paying attention, asking clarifying questions, and reflecting on what you have heard to ensure understanding. By actively listening, you show your partner their thoughts and feelings are valued, creating a safe space for open communication.

Another essential aspect of conflict resolution is seeking to understand before being understood. Instead of focusing solely on getting your point across, take the time to grasp where your partner is coming from. Empathy flourishes when we prioritize understanding each other's feelings and perspectives. When both parties feel heard and understood, it paves the way for meaningful resolutions that strengthen the relationship.

In conflicts, it's easy to get caught up in the desire to be right or to win the argument. However, shifting the focus from winning to understanding can lead to more productive outcomes. Empathy allows us to see beyond our viewpoints and consider the feelings and experiences of others. It encourages us to approach conflicts with a mindset of collaboration rather than competition.

By exploring techniques that enhance empathy and understanding in conflicts, we pave the way for healthier relationships built on mutual respect and compassion. Active listening and seeking to understand before being understood are powerful tools that can transform how we navigate disagreements with our partners. When prioritizing empathy in conflict resolution, we create space for deeper connections and foster an environment where both partners feel valued and understood.

Transforming Conflict Through Empathy and Understanding in Relationships

When conflicts arise in relationships, it's common to fall into the trap of wanting to win arguments rather than seeking to understand our partner's perspective. This shift in focus can lead to a breakdown in communication and a deepening of the conflict. However, by consciously redirecting our attention towards understanding our partner's point of view, we can pave the way for more effective conflict resolution and a healthier relationship overall.

Empathy plays a crucial role in this process. By actively listening to our partner without judgment and with genuine curiosity, we can gain valuable insights into their thoughts and feelings. This practice fosters understanding and demonstrates respect for their experiences and emotions. It shows that we value their perspective and are willing to engage in a dialogue acknowledging their reality.

In relationships, it's essential to remember that empathy is a two-way street. While we strive to understand our partner, we deserve the same understanding. By creating a mutual environment of empathy and compassion, conflicts can be approached with a collaborative mindset rather than a combative one. This shift in attitude can transform conflicts from battlegrounds into opportunities for growth and connection.

When prioritizing understanding over winning, we create space for vulnerability and openness in our relationships. Validation becomes a key component of this process, as acknowledging our partner's feelings and experiences helps them feel heard and valued. In turn, they are more likely to reciprocate this validation, fostering a cycle of empathy and support that strengthens the foundation of the relationship.

By shifting our focus from winning arguments to understanding partner perspectives, we lay the groundwork for effective conflict resolution and improved communication. This approach encourages emotional intelligence and compassion, nurturing a bond built on mutual respect and empathy. As we navigate conflicts with an open heart and mind, we pave the way for deeper connection and intimacy in our relationships.

Applying active listening and empathetic communication techniques can transform conflicts into opportunities for collaboration and understanding within relationships. By actively engaging in empathetic communication, partners can create a safe space for sharing thoughts and feelings, paving the way for deeper connection and mutual respect. Instead of focusing solely on being heard, the emphasis shifts towards truly understanding the other person's perspective.

Active listening involves more than just hearing words; it requires full engagement with the speaker's emotions and intentions. By giving undivided attention, maintaining eye contact, and mirroring back what is being said, couples can demonstrate genuine interest in understanding each other. This process fosters empathy and builds trust, which is essential for constructively resolving conflicts.

Empathetic communication involves acknowledging and validating the emotions expressed by one's partner. Rather than dismissing or downplaying feelings, partners should show empathy by recognizing the validity of those emotions. This practice creates a supportive environment where both individuals feel heard and valued.

To foster collaboration in conflict resolution, it is crucial to prioritize understanding over winning arguments. By setting aside the need to be right and instead focusing on comprehending each other's viewpoints, couples can work together towards finding mutually beneficial solutions. This approach cultivates a sense of teamwork and strengthens the bond between partners.

Encouraging open dialogue and active participation from both parties is key to effective conflict resolution. By creating a space where each person feels empowered to express themselves honestly without fear of judgment, couples can address underlying issues and work towards sustainable solutions. This collaborative effort promotes growth and resilience within the relationship.

Practicing patience and compassion during conflicts is essential for fostering a culture of empathy within a relationship. Partners can navigate challenges with grace and humility by approaching disagreements with understanding and kindness. This attitude diffuses tension and sets the stage for a deeper emotional connection.

Implementing active listening and empathetic communication

techniques requires dedication and practice but yields significant rewards in relationship satisfaction. By committing to these principles consistently, couples can nurture trust, build intimacy, and strengthen their bond over time. Investing in empathetic communication paves the way for enduring harmony and mutual support in adversity.

In summary, applying active listening and empathetic communication techniques transforms conflicts into opportunities for growth and connection within relationships. By prioritizing understanding, validation, and collaboration, couples can navigate disagreements with empathy and respect, fostering a deeper sense of unity and partnership.

Mastering empathy and understanding is not just a skill but a transformative approach that can redefine how conflicts are resolved in a relationship. By embracing techniques that enhance empathy, couples can move beyond the surface level of disputes and reach deeper, more meaningful resolutions that strengthen their bond. This shift from a mindset focused on winning arguments to one that prioritizes understanding your partner's perspective is crucial. It ensures that both individuals feel heard and valued, the cornerstone of a thriving relationship.

Active listening and empathetic communication are practical tools that facilitate this process. These methods allow you to genuinely engage with your partner's feelings and thoughts without judgment or defensiveness. This kind of communication fosters an environment where both partners can openly share their vulnerabilities and find common ground. The result is not just a resolution to a specific disagreement but an overall enhancement in the quality of the relationship.

Remember, the goal here is not merely to resolve conflicts as they arise but to cultivate a pattern of interaction that prevents many disputes from escalating in the first place. Couples can better understand each other's needs and expectations by applying these empathetic techniques consistently. This proactive approach alleviates stress and deepens intimacy, making each partner feel more connected and supported.

Taking control of how you handle conflict through empathy and understanding is empowering. It allows you to transform potential breakdowns into opportunities for growth and deeper connection. Each step taken towards empathetic communication is a step towards a more harmonious and fulfilling relationship. Therefore, engage actively with these strategies, embrace the process, and watch as your relationship transforms, fostering a loving environment where both partners thrive.

Chapter 8: Unraveling Relationship Tangles: Step-by-Step Resolutions

Are You Ready to Simplify the Complex Web of Relationship Challenges?

When couples face relationship difficulties, the path to resolution can often seem fraught with complexity and emotional turmoil. The overwhelming nature of intertwined issues can make even the most dedicated partners feel lost. Recognizing this, we aim to provide a clear, step-by-step approach that demystifies resolving these common challenges. The solution becomes clearer by breaking down issues into manageable parts, and couples gain the confidence to tackle problems together.

The Power of Simplicity

At its core, the essence of effective relationship problem-solving lies in simplifying what appears overwhelmingly complex. This chapter will guide you through learning how to dissect these large issues into smaller, more manageable components. This methodology doesn't just clarify the problems; it also illuminates the path to solutions. Each step forward is designed to rebuild confidence and restore control to both partners.

Building Confidence Through Clarity

A significant benefit of adopting a step-by-step approach is the **boost in confidence** it provides. Couples feel more empowered When they understand what's going wrong and see a clear route to improvement. This chapter aims not only to guide but also to reassure you that issues can indeed be resolved with patience and persistence. It's about transforming the daunting task of 'fixing a relationship' into an achievable series of steps.

Therapy as a Tool, Not a Crutch

Often, therapy is viewed as a last resort or a sign that the relationship has reached its crisis point. However, redefining therapy as a practical tool for everyday problems is crucial. Here, we'll explore how therapy can be integrated into your regular relationship maintenance routine, helping you address issues before they escalate. Understanding therapy as an accessible resource can fundamentally change how couples approach relationship care.

Action Over Contemplation

The emphasis on action is pivotal. While understanding and discussing relationship dynamics are important, this chapter encourages *active engagement* with practical solutions. It's about moving from passive understanding to active resolution—implementing strategies that produce real changes in your relationship dynamics.

Empowerment Through Emotional Mastery

Another key aspect we'll cover is emotional mastery—how you can harness your emotions to foster rather than hinder your relationship's healing and growth. Emotional reactions are often automatic, but couples can learn to manage their responses constructively with the right tools and awareness.

This chapter provides hope and tangible pathways toward healthier and more fulfilling relationships by focusing on these elements. It empowers readers with knowledge and techniques that turn daunting challenges into surmountable tasks, encouraging them to take control and actively engage in their journey toward revived love.

This structured yet compassionate approach ensures that each step is informed and intentional, aiming for lasting improvements in communication and intimacy within relationships.

In relationships, problems can often feel overwhelming and impossible. Getting caught up in complex issues is common, leading to helplessness and frustration. However, by learning to break down these complex issues into manageable steps, you can regain control and clarity in addressing them. A step-by-step approach to unraveling relationship tangles can make the process more manageable and less daunting.

One key aspect of breaking down complex issues is identifying the root cause. Rather than getting lost in the web of symptoms and surface-level conflicts, it's crucial to delve deeper and pinpoint the underlying issues contributing to your challenges. By understanding the core reasons behind your relationship struggles, you can develop targeted solutions that address the root of the problem.

Communication plays a pivotal role in untangling relationship knots. Open and honest dialogue between partners is essential for gaining insights into each other's perspectives, feelings, and needs. When discussing complex issues, listening actively, expressing yourself clearly, and validating your partner's emotions are important. Effective communication lays the foundation for constructive problem-solving and paves the way for deeper understanding and connection.

Setting realistic goals is another crucial step in breaking down complex relationship issues. By establishing achievable objectives, you create a roadmap for progress and prevent feelings of overwhelm or stagnation. Start small by focusing on specific aspects of the problem that you can address incrementally rather than tackling everything at once. Celebrate each milestone, reinforcing your motivation and commitment to working through challenges together.

Seeking support from a therapist or counselor can provide invaluable guidance in navigating complex relationship issues. A trained professional can offer impartial insights, practical tools, and a safe space for exploring difficult emotions and dynamics within your relationship. Therapy can help you gain new perspectives, learn effective communication techniques, and develop strategies for resolving conflicts constructively.

Building Confidence in Addressing Common Relationship Challenges

In addressing and resolving common relationship challenges, gaining confidence is key to navigating the complexities. Confidence in one's ability to tackle issues head-on can significantly impact the outcome of discussions and resolutions within a relationship. Individuals must recognize their strengths and trust their capacity to overcome obstacles together.

Communication, as always, plays a pivotal role in addressing challenges. Expressing thoughts, emotions, and concerns openly and honestly is fundamental in resolving conflicts. Encouraging partners to listen actively and empathetically can lead to a deeper understanding of each other's perspectives, fostering a more harmonious environment for conflict resolution.

Conflict resolution skills are like any other; they can be honed and improved with practice. By approaching challenges with an open mind and a willingness to find common ground, couples can navigate disagreements more effectively. Focusing on solutions is essential rather than getting caught up in the problem.

Taking responsibility for one's actions and reactions is another vital aspect of resolving relationship challenges. Acknowledging mistakes and learning from them shows maturity and a commitment to personal growth within the relationship. This level of self-awareness can pave the way for healthier interactions moving forward.

In addressing common relationship challenges, couples must remember they are a team. Teamwork involves supporting each other through difficulties, celebrating victories, and facing obstacles as a united front. This sense of unity can strengthen the bond between partners and create a solid foundation for overcoming future challenges.

Patience is a virtue when it comes to resolving relationship issues. Real change takes time, effort, and dedication. By setting realistic expectations and being patient with each other's progress, couples can work towards sustainable solutions that promote long-term harmony in their relationship.

Ultimately, gaining confidence in addressing common

relationship challenges involves effective communication, active listening, conflict resolution skills, personal responsibility, teamwork, patience, and, most importantly, a deep commitment to the partnership. By embracing these principles and practices, couples can navigate even the most intricate tangles in their relationships with clarity and resilience.

Analytical Framework

For navigating relationship challenges effectively, the Analytical Framework provides a structured approach to problem-solving. Problem identification is the initial step, allowing couples to articulate issues without blame and fostering a shared understanding. Moving to the analysis phase, problems are deconstructed into emotional triggers, behavioral patterns, unmet needs, and external influences. This phase helps in gaining clarity on the root causes of conflicts.

The solution generation phase encourages couples to brainstorm ideas with empathy, creativity, and practicality. Collaborative decision-making ensures that both partners are actively involved in finding solutions. Each potential solution is then evaluated for feasibility, considering possible outcomes, available resources, and barriers to implementation.

Solution selection and implementation form the final phases of the framework. Couples choose a solution together, plan its execution, and monitor its effectiveness. An iterative review allows adjustments based on real-world results, ensuring adaptability. Tools like structured problem-solving worksheets and decision matrices aid in implementing solutions effectively.

This framework's components interact synergistically to guide couples through a systematic conflict resolution process. The dynamics involve a continuous feedback loop where each phase informs and refines the next, creating a structured path toward relationship improvement over time.

This model empowers couples to tackle issues collaboratively, promoting mutual understanding and shared responsibility in problem-solving. Providing a clear roadmap with actionable steps, the Analytical Framework equips partners with the tools to address challenges methodically and effectively.

The Analytical Framework offers a structured approach to relationship problem-solving by breaking down complex issues into manageable parts. Through iterative processes and collaborative decision-making, couples can navigate conflicts with clarity and purpose, fostering growth and strengthening their bond over time.

The Path to Empowerment: A Step-by-Step Guide to Resolving Relationship Challenges

Navigating the complexities of relationship tangles can be daunting, but by breaking these challenges into manageable steps, couples can confidently approach them and see meaningful progress. This guide simplifies the process and empowers you and your partner to use therapy as a practical tool for growth and connection.

Step 1: Breaking Down Complex Issues into Manageable Steps

Firstly, identify a specific issue that's been a source of conflict or misunderstanding. Analyze the underlying factors contributing to this challenge and break it into smaller, more digestible components. Prioritize these components and create an action plan with clear, achievable steps. Set realistic timelines for each step, allowing flexibility to adjust as you progress. This structured approach demystifies the problem-solving process, making it less overwhelming and more actionable.

Step 2: Gaining Confidence in Addressing and Resolving Common Relationship Challenges

As you execute your action plan, maintain a positive mindset. Your confidence will grow with each small victory, reinforcing your capability to handle relationship challenges. Apply therapeutic techniques discussed earlier to navigate these issues effectively. Support from your partner is crucial; lean on each other for motivation and celebrate every success together, reinforcing the teamwork needed to build a stronger bond.

Step 3: Viewing Therapy as a Practical Tool for Effective Problem-Solving

Therapy should be seen as a remedy for crises and a staple in your relationship maintenance toolkit. Embrace it as a means to address and preempt potential conflicts regularly. Utilize recommended resources like workbooks or online tools to enhance your problem-solving skills. Remember, engaging in therapy is a proactive measure that fosters a healthier, more joyful relationship.

This step-by-step guide doesn't just offer a method to tackle relationship issues—it provides a roadmap to deeper understanding and renewed connection. By embracing these strategies, you empower yourselves to resolve current challenges and equip yourselves with the tools needed for future hurdles. This proactive approach ensures that both partners feel heard, valued, and connected, paving the way for a revitalized partnership.

Chapter 9: Knowing Us, Knowing You: The Power of Self-Assessment

"In all the world, there is no heart for me like yours.

In all the world, there is no love

for you like mine."

Maya Angelou

Unlock the Secrets to a Stronger Relationship Through Self-Assessment

In any meaningful relationship, understanding each other is as crucial as understanding oneself. This chapter delves into the transformative potential of self-assessment tools that can catalyze connections and foster deeper intimacy. By embracing quizzes and questionnaires, couples can uncover layers of their relationship dynamics that often go unnoticed yet significantly influence their interactions and emotional bonds.

Self-assessment tools are more than just a checklist of dos and don'ts; they are mirrors reflecting your relationship's true state from various angles. These tools provide **valuable insights** into personal attitudes, behaviors, and preferences, highlighting how these elements mesh or clash within the partnership. You and your partner can decide where to focus your energies to enhance your relationship by identifying strengths and weaknesses.

Embrace the Journey of Personal Discovery

Fostering self-awareness is an ongoing process that does not end with knowing your favorite color or whether you prefer coffee over tea. It involves deeply exploring one's motivations, fears, desires, and behavioral patterns. Self-assessment in a relationship context magnifies this process by including the dynamics between you and your partner. It's about uncovering how individual traits affect shared life scenarios and how they can be harmonized for a healthier relationship.

Building Blocks for Lasting Change

Implementing regular self-assessments allows couples to track their growth over time and adapt to life's inevitable changes. Tools like quizzes help set a baseline to measure progress in communication styles, conflict resolution strategies, and mutual understanding. This continuous improvement is not just about fixing what's broken but nurturing what works well and discovering new areas for growth together.

Integrating assessment tools into your routine encourages ongoing dialogue about each partner's needs and expectations and opens avenues for continuous personal development and relational enhancement. This proactive approach helps maintain the vitality of your connection, keeping the romantic spark alive even in long-term relationships.

Actionable Steps Towards Improvement

The insights gained from these assessments should translate into actionable strategies tailored to address specific aspects of your relationship. Whether it's learning to communicate more effectively, managing disagreements with compassion and understanding, or enhancing emotional connections, each step forward is designed to solidify the foundation of your partnership.

Engaging with these tools is not a one-time activity but a vital part of a sustained effort to deepen intimacy and ensure both partners feel valued and understood. Through this systematic exploration, couples can transform challenges into stepping stones toward a more fulfilling union.

By the end of this chapter, you will have gained a clearer view of where your relationship stands and practical tools for ongoing enhancement. This journey of mutual discovery is essential for any couple looking to continuously revive their love and commitment. The power of self-assessment lies in its ability to illuminate paths forward together—a truly invaluable asset in any loving relationship.

Self-assessment tools serve as valuable resources in evaluating the strengths and weaknesses of a relationship. These quizzes and questionnaires provide couples with a structured way to reflect on their dynamics, communication styles, and areas needing improvement. Self-assessment lets Partners gain insights into their relationship patterns, triggers, and preferences. This process allows for a more objective view of the relationship, enabling individuals to identify areas where they excel and aspects that could benefit from attention.

Assessing relationship strengths is crucial for acknowledging the positive aspects of the partnership. It helps couples recognize what works well, fostering appreciation and gratitude for each other's contributions. Understanding these strengths can boost confidence in the relationship and serve as a foundation for growth and development. Individuals can leverage these qualities to navigate challenges more effectively and deepen their connection by pinpointing what makes the partnership strong.

Conversely, evaluating relationship weaknesses is equally important in fostering growth and improvement. Identifying areas of concern or recurring issues allows couples to address underlying problems proactively. It opens up opportunities for constructive conversations about how to overcome obstacles together. Recognizing weaknesses does not signify failure but rather highlights areas that require attention and effort to enhance the overall quality of the relationship.

Fostering Self-Awareness for Personal Growth and Relationship Development

Self-awareness is a crucial component of personal growth and development within a relationship. By fostering self-awareness through assessment tools, individuals can gain valuable insights into their behaviors, emotions, and thinking patterns. These tools serve as mirrors, reflecting aspects of ourselves that may be difficult to see without external feedback. Self-awareness allows us to recognize our strengths and weaknesses, providing a solid foundation for personal growth and improvement.

One powerful aspect of utilizing assessment tools for self-awareness is the ability to identify areas where we may need to make changes or adjustments. Recognizing our patterns and tendencies can highlight areas where we might contribute to conflicts or misunderstandings within the relationship. By acknowledging these aspects of ourselves, we can take proactive steps towards personal development and growth.

Assessment tools also offer the opportunity for individuals to deepen their understanding of their own emotions and reactions. By exploring our emotional responses, we can understand why we react in certain ways in specific situations. This awareness enables us to respond more intentionally than impulsively, improving communication and conflict resolution within the relationship.

Furthermore, self-assessment tools encourage individuals to take ownership of their growth journey. Empowering individuals to engage in self-reflection and introspection actively fosters a sense of control over their development. This sense of agency can motivate individuals to make positive changes and strive for continuous improvement.

Incorporating assessment tools into a regular practice of self-reflection can lead to profound personal transformation. By regularly evaluating our thoughts, feelings, and behaviors, we create opportunities for growth and evolution. This ongoing process of self-assessment benefits the individual and enriches the relationship as each partner becomes more self-aware and attuned to their own needs and those of their partner.

Ultimately, fostering self-awareness through assessment tools is a dynamic process that requires commitment and dedication. It is a journey of self-discovery that can lead to greater clarity, understanding, and fulfillment within oneself and in the context of the relationship. Embracing this process wholeheartedly can pave the way for meaningful personal development and enhanced relational dynamics based on mutual understanding and growth.

Driving Continuous Improvement in Your Relationship

Now that you have gained valuable insights into your relationship dynamics and personal growth through self-assessment tools, it's time to drive continuous improvements in your relationship based on these newfound understandings. Harness the power of self-awareness to make intentional changes and foster a deeper connection with your partner.

- Communication is Key: Use assessment information to open dialogue with your partner. Share your reflections, strengths, weaknesses, and areas for improvement in a constructive and non-confrontational manner. Encourage open communication by actively listening to your partner's feedback and concerns.

- Set Mutual Goals: Based on the insights gained from self-assessments, work with your partner to establish shared goals for personal and relationship growth. These goals can focus on communication, conflict resolution, intimacy, or individual development. You strengthen your bond and motivation for positive change by aligning your aspirations.

- Implement Actionable Strategies: Translate your goals into actionable steps you and your partner can take to drive progress in your relationship. Whether scheduling regular date nights, attending couples therapy sessions, or practicing active listening techniques, commit to concrete actions that support your shared objectives.

- Celebrate Progress: Acknowledge and celebrate the small victories along the way. Recognize your and your partner's efforts towards positive change and growth. Acknowledging progress reinforces your commitment to continuous improvement and motivates others to keep moving forward.

- Seek Support When Needed: Don't hesitate to seek external support if challenges arise or you feel stuck in your progress. Whether it's reaching out to a therapist, joining a support group, or seeking guidance from a mentor, external resources can provide valuable insights and guidance as you navigate the journey of self-discovery and relationship enhancement.

- Embrace Flexibility: Remember that growth is a dynamic process that requires flexibility and adaptability. Be open to adjusting your strategies and goals as you learn more about yourself and your partner. Embracing change with an open mind fosters resilience and strengthens the foundation of your relationship.

- Practice Gratitude: Cultivate a sense of gratitude for the progress you've made together—express appreciation for each other's efforts, support, and commitment to growth. Gratitude enhances emotional connection and reinforces the positive changes you are making in your relationship.

By leveraging self-assessment tools to drive continuous improvements in your relationship, you pave the way for deeper understanding, connection, and fulfillment with your partner. Stay committed to personal growth, open communication, and mutual support as you navigate the path toward a more enriching partnership.

The journey of relationship enhancement through self-assessment is both enlightening and essential. By integrating quizzes, questionnaires, and other assessment tools, couples gain valuable insights into the dynamics of their partnership. These tools are not just evaluation methods but catalysts for deeper understanding and growth. They empower each partner to recognize their strengths and areas where they can improve, making every insight a stepping stone toward a stronger bond.

Continuous personal development is crucial in any relationship. Self-assessment tools encourage partners to maintain a proactive approach towards personal growth and mutual understanding. This ongoing development is vital for keeping the relationship dynamic and resilient against life's challenges. Remember, as individuals grow, so does the relationship.

Assessing and addressing relationship dynamics should be seen as an opportunity for renewal and deepening connections rather than a critique. Based on these insights, each step brings couples closer, helping them navigate their journey with more empathy and support. This proactive stance helps preemptively manage potential conflicts and enhance the joy shared between partners.

Embrace these tools with an open heart and mind. Let them guide you through a transformative journey where both partners feel valued and understood. Your active participation and willingness to explore the depths of your relationship will lead to a more fulfilling and enduring partnership.

Remember, the goal here is not perfection but progress. Every small step you take based on your assessments contributes significantly to the health and happiness of your relationship. Engage with these strategies, discuss the outcomes openly, and let them lead you to a path of continuous connection and rediscovery in your partnership.

Chapter 10: Reclaiming Connection: Strategies Against Digital Overload

"Love is when the other person's happiness

is more important than your own."

H. Jackson Brown Jr.

Are You a Screen Slave? Reclaim Your Relationship from Digital Clutches

In an era dominated by digital devices, the quality of personal relationships is silently eroding. It's not just about the time spent staring at screens but about what we miss during those hours—meaningful, face-to-face interactions vital for nurturing relationships. This chapter explores how consciously reducing screen time can significantly enhance communication and deepen bonds between partners.

Understanding Screen Time Impact

The first crucial step is recognizing the impact of excessive digital engagement on relationship health. Many couples may not immediately link their relationship dissatisfaction to the pervasive presence of technology. However, research consistently highlights a negative correlation between screen time and relationship quality. By acknowledging this, couples can take proactive steps towards change.

Embracing Digital Detox

Implementing digital detox strategies is more than just turning off notifications or setting aside phones during dinner. It involves a holistic approach to managing technology so that it serves us without enslaving us. Strategies, like designated tech-free hours and partner agreements can foster healthier interactions and ensure both individuals feel valued and heard.

Fostering Real Connection

Beyond reducing screen time, engaging in practices that actively strengthen face-to-face interactions is essential. Quality conversations, shared activities, and physical closeness are nurtured through undistracted time together. This chapter will guide you through setting up routines and rituals that encourage direct communication and deepen emotional connections, helping couples reclaim intimacy from technology's clutches.

Our devices often dictate our attention and shape our relationships in this digital age. By controlling how and when we use technology, we empower ourselves to improve the quality of our connections with those we love.

Reclaiming connection in your relationship doesn't require radical changes or complete abandonment of digital devices. Instead, it calls for mindful adjustments and a commitment to prioritize one another over screens. Through practical steps and achievable strategies, couples can rediscover the joys of truly being together in the present moment.

Let this guide you to balance your digital life with your romantic life, ensuring that technology enhances rather than dictates your relationship dynamics. Take these first steps towards a renewed connection with your partner, where every moment spent together is meaningful and cherished.

Excessive screen time can significantly impact the quality of your relationships. In a world where digital devices often take precedence over face-to-face interactions, the depth and intimacy of connections can suffer. When phones, tablets, or computers become constant companions, meaningful conversations and shared moments can be overshadowed. The constant distraction of screens can diminish the quality of communication between partners, leading to feelings of disconnect and isolation. Recognizing this impact is the first step towards reclaiming the essence of genuine connection in your relationship.

When screens dominate our attention during shared moments, they are barriers to true engagement and emotional connection. Partners may find themselves physically present but mentally absent, absorbed in social media feeds or responding to work emails instead of actively participating in conversations or activities with their loved ones. This can lead to neglect or disinterest within the relationship, eroding the foundation of trust and emotional intimacy that sustains a healthy partnership.

Moreover, excessive screen time can foster a culture of instant gratification and shallow interactions, where quick messages or emojis replace heartfelt conversations and meaningful gestures. The depth of emotional expression may be compromised when reduced to text messages or brief online exchanges, depriving relationships of the richness of genuine face-to-face communication. This shift towards superficial connections can leave partners feeling unfulfilled and disconnected, longing for the authentic engagement that only direct interaction can provide.

By acknowledging the negative impact of excessive screen time on relationship quality, you empower yourself to take proactive steps toward reclaiming deeper connections with your partner. Recognizing when screens hinder meaningful interactions allows you to prioritize moments of undivided attention and genuine engagement with your loved one. Through intentional efforts to limit digital distractions and focus on quality time together, you can cultivate an environment where open communication and emotional closeness flourish.

Reclaiming Meaningful Communication in the Digital Age

In today's digital age, getting caught up in the constant stream of notifications, messages, and social media updates is easy. This can lead to decreased quality time spent with our partners, affecting the depth of our connections. However, there are simple yet effective strategies that can help us reclaim meaningful communication and enhance our relationships.

- Setting Boundaries: One crucial step in implementing a digital detox is setting boundaries around screen time. Designate specific times when devices are put away during the day, allowing for uninterrupted one-on-one interaction with your partner. Establishing these boundaries creates space for deeper conversations and shared experiences without distractions.

- Tech-Free Zones: Designating certain areas in your home as tech-free zones can also help reduce screen time and promote face-to-face interaction. For example, consider making the dining table or the bedroom a device-free space where you can focus on each other without the interference of screens. This simple adjustment can significantly improve the quality of your interactions.

- Engage in Shared Activities: Instead of spending time on individual screens, prioritize engaging in shared activities that foster connection. Whether cooking a meal together, walking, or playing a board game, finding activities that both partners enjoy can strengthen your bond and create lasting memories. These shared experiences help build intimacy and deepen your connection.

- Practice Active Listening: In a world filled with distractions, practicing active listening is a powerful way to show your partner that you value their thoughts and feelings. Put away your devices, make eye contact, and give them your full attention when they speak. Active listening fosters understanding and empathy, strengthening the foundation of your relationship.

- Schedule Quality Time: Just as we schedule appointments and meetings, prioritizing quality time with your partner is essential for maintaining a strong connection. Block out time in your calendar for date nights or activities that allow you to focus solely on each other. By intentionally spending quality time together, you reinforce the importance of your relationship.

- Express Gratitude: Taking time to express gratitude for each other can significantly impact the quality of your relationship. Make it a habit to share what you appreciate about your partner regularly. Expressing gratitude cultivates positivity and reinforces mutual appreciation, creating a supportive and loving environment for both partners.

- Embrace Offline Communication: While digital communication has benefits, nothing beats face-to-face interaction when building intimacy. Make an effort to have meaningful conversations without screens present. Direct communication allows for deeper connections and fosters emotional closeness between partners.

Implementing these practical strategies and prioritizing quality time with your partner can combat digital overload and strengthen your relationship. Remember that small changes can lead to significant improvements in communication and connection. Reclaiming meaningful interactions is essential for nurturing a healthy and fulfilling relationship.

In the quest to strengthen face-to-face interactions and deepen relationship bonds, it is essential to prioritize quality time together. Setting aside dedicated moments for direct communication can work wonders in rekindling intimacy and fostering a deeper connection with your partner. Make a conscious effort to engage in meaningful conversations without distractions, allowing each other the undivided attention needed to understand and connect on a deeper level.

Embrace shared activities that promote bonding and create lasting memories. Whether cooking a meal together, walking, or engaging in a hobby you enjoy, these shared experiences can enhance your emotional connection and build a sense of unity within your relationship. By focusing on activities that bring joy and fulfillment, you are actively investing in the strength of your bond.

Practice active listening to show your partner their thoughts, feelings, and opinions are valued. Avoid interrupting and truly listen with empathy and understanding. Reflecting what you have heard can demonstrate your commitment to mutual respect and communication. This simple yet powerful technique can pave the way for open, honest dialogue that deepens your emotional connection.

Express gratitude and appreciation for your partner regularly. Acknowledging their efforts, kindness, and presence in your life can cultivate a sense of warmth and positivity in your relationship. Small gestures of gratitude go a long way in reinforcing the bond between you and nurturing feelings of love and appreciation.

Create rituals of connection that are unique to your relationship. Whether it's a weekly date night, a morning coffee together, or a bedtime routine that involves sharing highlights of the day, these rituals can provide stability and comfort while fostering intimacy. Consistency in these rituals can serve as anchors in your relationship, grounding you both in moments of togetherness.

Prioritize physical touch as a means of non-verbal communication. Hugs, kisses, holding hands, and other forms of affectionate touch can convey love, support, and reassurance without needing words. Physical intimacy is crucial in deepening emotional connections and maintaining closeness between partners.

Seek growth opportunities together by exploring new experiences or learning new skills as a couple. Engaging in activities that challenge you can strengthen your bond through shared achievements and mutual support—embracing growth as a couple fosters resilience and unity in facing life's challenges.

By implementing these strategies to strengthen face-to-face interactions and deepen relationship bonds, you are actively investing in the health and vitality of your partnership. Remember that meaningful connections require effort, intentionality, and genuine care for each other's well-being. Through consistently practicing these strategies, you can cultivate a relationship filled with love, understanding, and enduring connection.

Embrace Simplicity, Enhance Connection

The journey toward revitalizing your relationship by managing digital influences is both necessary and rewarding. Recognizing the detrimental impact of excessive screen time is the first critical step. It is clear that when screens dominate our attention, the quality of our interactions suffers. This realization is not about fostering guilt but inspiring action towards healthier habits.

Implementing digital detox strategies is more than just turning off devices; it's about reclaiming the moments that truly matter. These practical strategies are designed to fit seamlessly into your daily life, ensuring you can start making changes immediately. Whether it's designating tech-free zones in your home or setting specific times to unplug, each step contributes significantly to enhancing the quality of your interactions.

The power of face-to-face communication cannot be overstated. By strengthening these direct interactions, you deepen the emotional connection with your partner. This doesn't require grand gestures but simply the commitment to be present. Listening intently, sharing openly, and engaging fully are foundational to rebuilding and maintaining a strong, intimate bond.

You can steer the course of your relationship away from digital distractions and towards enriched, meaningful communication. Each small change in managing technology's role in your life paves the way for more profound connections. Embrace these strategies with an open heart and a willing mind, and witness your relationship dynamic transform. Remember, the most significant moments often arise from the simplest exchanges.

Let this chapter serve as a gentle reminder and a practical guide in your journey toward a more connected and fulfilling relationship. The steps outlined here are not just suggestions but essential actions for anyone looking to thrive in their connections amidst the digital age. Your efforts to engage in meaningful communication will undoubtedly be rewarded with a stronger, more resilient bond with your loved one.

Chapter 11: Beyond the Basics: Extending Relationship Learning

"The best and most beautiful things in this world

cannot be seen or even heard but must be

felt with the heart."

Helen Keller

Unveiling New Dimensions in Your Relationship Journey

Embarking on a journey of relationship rejuvenation through a couple's therapy is courageous and rewarding. This chapter aims to broaden that horizon, offering various resources and perspectives that deepen your understanding and enhance your connection. By integrating these tools, couples can reinforce what they've learned and discover new strategies to nurture their relationship.

Extending Your Toolkit with Guided Reading

The landscape of couple's therapy is vast and rich with varied approaches and insights. Here, we will introduce a curated reading list designed to complement and expand upon the foundational techniques discussed earlier in this book. These resources have been carefully selected to address common relationship challenges, providing theoretical knowledge and practical applications. Couples can better understand each other's emotional landscapes by engaging with these readings, leading to deeper empathy and stronger bonds.

Broadening Perspectives Through Diverse Resources

It's crucial to recognize that no single approach fits all when healing and strengthening a relationship. Therefore, this chapter also connects you with a broader range of tools—from digital apps designed to enhance daily communication to workshops and seminars that offer immersive experiences. Exploring these tools allows couples to tailor their path to improvement, choosing strategies that resonate most with their unique situation and personalities.

Engaging Actively for Lasting Change

The final key element we discuss here is the importance of active engagement with the recommended materials. Passive reading is informative, but the true transformation comes from applying what you learn directly to your relationship. This section will guide you on effectively integrating insights into your daily interactions, ensuring that every piece of knowledge acquired translates into real-world benefits.

Couples can transform their understanding into action by embracing these extended learning opportunities. This proactive approach reinforces the therapeutic concepts discussed and empowers individuals within the relationship to become agents of change.

In navigating these expanded resources, remember that each step taken is part of a larger journey towards rekindling connection. There are many paths, but the destination remains the same: a revitalized, loving partnership where both individuals feel understood, appreciated, and deeply connected.

Embrace this chapter as your gateway to exploring new dimensions in your relationship, armed with the best tools and knowledge available. With each page turned and each strategy applied, you are crafting a stronger foundation for a lifetime of love and happiness together.

In couples therapy, delving deeper into additional resources and reading lists can significantly enhance your understanding and application of therapeutic techniques. These resources serve as invaluable companions on your journey toward relationship improvement, offering insights, strategies, and perspectives that complement the foundational knowledge gained from this book. Exploring a broader range of tools and perspectives opens new pathways for personal growth and relational enrichment.

Extending your learning beyond the basics of couple's therapy involves immersing yourself in a wealth of knowledge available through recommended reading materials. These resources are carefully curated to provide diverse viewpoints, practical exercises, and expert guidance to deepen your grasp of therapeutic concepts. Engaging with these materials reinforces the teachings presented in this book and empowers you to explore various approaches to strengthen your relationship dynamics.

Reading lists tailored to enhance a couple's therapy offers a treasure trove of wisdom waiting to be uncovered. From renowned experts to personal accounts of triumph over relationship challenges, each recommended resource provides a unique perspective on fostering connection, improving communication, and nurturing intimacy. By immersing yourself in these texts, you gain a wellspring of knowledge that can transform your approach to relational issues and pave the way for lasting positive change.

Exploring additional resources equips you with a broader toolkit for navigating the complexities of relationships. Each book or article recommended serves as a beacon of insight, illuminating areas where growth is possible and offering practical strategies for overcoming obstacles. Expanding your reading list and embracing diverse perspectives will enrich your understanding of the nuances within couple dynamics and empower you to implement transformative practices in your relationship.

Embracing Diversity in Tools and Perspectives

In your journey towards rekindling connection in your relationship, you must broaden your toolbox with diverse tools and perspectives for improvement. Connecting with different approaches can offer fresh insights and strategies, empowering you to navigate challenges more effectively. Delving into various resources and techniques opens up new avenues for growth and transformation in your relationship.

Diversity in tools and perspectives enriches your understanding of the complex dynamics at play within a relationship. Each approach brings a unique lens to view interactions, communication patterns, and emotional responses. Exploring these diverse viewpoints can help you gain a more comprehensive grasp of your relationship dynamics and identify areas for improvement.

Engaging with a broader range of tools fosters creativity in problem-solving. When faced with obstacles or conflicts, having multiple strategies at your disposal allows you to adapt and tailor your approach to suit the situation. Creativity fosters innovation within your relationship, enabling you to explore new ways of communicating, connecting, and resolving issues.

Different perspectives provide fresh insights into familiar challenges. By stepping outside your usual frame of reference, you may discover alternative ways of interpreting situations or approaching conflicts. These new insights can spark growth and encourage you to break free from unproductive patterns that may have been holding your relationship back.

Embracing various tools and perspectives encourages flexibility in your approach to relationship improvement. Just as every individual is unique, every relationship is distinct, requiring adaptable strategies that can evolve alongside the changing dynamics between partners. Flexibility empowers you to respond effectively to the ebbs and flows of your relationship journey.

Connecting with a broader range of tools and perspectives demonstrates a commitment to your relationship's ongoing growth and enrichment. Embracing resource diversity deepens your understanding and strengthens your bond as a couple. Through exploration and engagement with various approaches, you pave the way for lasting transformation and connection in your relationship.

Engaging with recommended materials that reinforce therapeutic concepts can significantly enhance your understanding and application of the strategies discussed in this book. By delving into these resources, you can deepen your learning and solidify the foundation for improving your relationship.

Reading suggested books and articles or attending workshops

related to couples therapy can offer valuable insights and practical techniques that complement the principles outlined in this guide. These additional resources extend the concepts presented here, giving you a broader perspective on relationship dynamics and communication strategies.

Reinforcing your knowledge through supplementary materials allows you to explore different approaches and perspectives, enriching your understanding of navigating challenges and fostering intimacy in your relationship. By immersing yourself in these resources, you can gain new tools and strategies to address specific issues or enhance areas where you seek improvement.

Engaging with recommended materials also reinforces the importance of ongoing learning and growth within a relationship. It demonstrates your commitment to evolving as a couple and investing in the well-being of your partnership. By actively seeking additional resources, you show dedication to nurturing a healthy and fulfilling connection with your partner.

By extending your learning beyond the basics, you open yourself up to a world of knowledge and expertise that can empower you to overcome obstacles and strengthen the bond with your significant other. These materials support your journey toward deeper connection, effective communication, and lasting intimacy.

Consider creating a reading list or schedule for exploring these recommended materials systematically. Setting aside dedicated time to engage with these resources can help you integrate their teachings into your daily life and relationship practices.

Remember, consistent effort and a willingness to learn are key to successful relationship growth.

Don't underestimate the power of supplementary resources in reinforcing the concepts discussed in this book. They serve as valuable tools in expanding your skills and understanding, ultimately leading to a more harmonious and fulfilling relationship. Embrace the opportunity to delve deeper into relationship dynamics through these recommended materials.

As you embark on this extended learning journey, keep an open mind and be willing to experiment with new ideas and approaches. Each resource has the potential to offer unique insights that can contribute to the enrichment of your relationship. Approach this process with curiosity and a sense of exploration, knowing that every bit of knowledge gained brings you closer to a stronger, more connected partnership.

Throughout this discussion, we have emphasized the significance of expanding your learning horizon beyond the immediate therapy sessions. By delving into additional resources and reading lists, you are not just passively absorbing information but actively engaging in your journey toward a healthier, more resilient relationship.

The tools and perspectives we have explored together offer a rich tapestry of knowledge that can be tailored to fit the unique dynamics of your partnership. Remember, each relationship is distinct, and the more tools you have at your disposal, the better equipped you are to navigate its complexities. Engaging with various materials reinforces the concepts discussed and brings new life into your understanding and applying these ideas.

Recognizing that these resources are designed to be practical and applicable in everyday life is crucial. They are not merely academic exercises but are steps towards profound personal and relational growth. Integrating these tools into daily interactions sets a foundation for continual improvement and deeper intimacy.

You have the innate ability to transform your relationship. Each resource recommended in this chapter serves as a stepping stone toward achieving a more fulfilling connection with your partner. Embrace these opportunities with openness and curiosity, and let them guide you to a deeper understanding of each other.

Remember, the path to improvement is always in motion. Keep drawing on these resources and refining your skills as you move forward. Your commitment to this process is not just beneficial—it's transformative. By taking control and actively participating in your relationship's growth, you are paving the way for lasting love and understanding.

Your journey doesn't end here. Let these resources inspire you to explore further and challenge yourself continuously. Your effort today will lay the groundwork for the thriving relationship you aspire to cultivate.

Chapter 12: Keeping Hope Alive: The Role of Encouragement

"When you stop expecting people to be perfect,

you can like them for who they are."

Donald Miller

Unleashing the Power of Encouragement in Relationships

When traversing the often tumultuous journey of relationship therapy, understanding the **importance of motivation** and encouragement cannot be overstated. Couples aspiring to rekindle their connection face myriad challenges, from confronting painful truths to adapting new communication techniques. Maintaining hope and a positive outlook in this environment is crucial for progress and the relationship's survival.

Motivation: The Bedrock of Progress

Motivation in couples therapy is as dynamic as the individuals involved. It can soar during breakthrough moments and plummet during stress or discord. Herein lies the profound value of encouragement: it serves as a consistent, gentle reminder that progress—though sometimes slow—is indeed happening. The strategic placement of encouragement notes throughout this guide acts as small beacons of light, guiding couples through their darkest hours and reinforcing their commitment to each other.

Fostering a Hopeful Reading Environment

Creating a supportive reading environment is more than just providing information; crafting an experience uplifting and motivating. Through encouragement notes, we introduce a layer of interactive engagement that personalizes the therapy journey. These notes are designed to resonate with you, offering timely words of affirmation that validate your efforts and reassure you that your struggles are not in vain.

The Optimistic Outlook

Maintaining an optimistic outlook is essential for mental and emotional health and the practical success of relationship therapy. Optimism helps us envision a future where problems are resolved and effort leads to improvement. It allows us to approach each therapy session with open hearts and minds—ready to tackle tough issues without fear or reservation.

The use yet simplicity of encouragement notes can significantly amplify this effect. They remind us that every small step forward is a victory worth celebrating. This positive reinforcement helps sustain motivation over time, making it easier for couples to engage deeply with therapeutic processes even when they feel overwhelmed or discouraged.

Actionable Strategies for Emotional Mastery

The power to change your relationship dynamics lies within your hands; understanding how to harness it is what we aim to equip you with in this discussion. By actively integrating encouragement into your therapy routine—through written notes, verbal affirmations, or thoughtful gestures—you create a self-sustaining positive feedback cycle that boosts both partners' morale.

This chapter will guide you through practical ways to implement these strategies effectively. You'll learn how simple encouragement can lead to profound shifts in attitude and behavior within your relationship. Moreover, these strategies are designed to be easy to implement yet impactful, ensuring you can apply them immediately.

By fostering an environment rich with support and optimism, you are laying down the foundational stones upon which lasting love and connection can be rebuilt. Remember, every word of encouragement is a step towards a brighter future together; let's take those steps confidently and see where they lead us.

Understanding the pivotal role of motivation and encouragement in relationship therapy is crucial for progress and growth. Motivation can ebb and flow in the journey toward revitalizing a connection, making it essential to harness the power of encouragement to sustain momentum. Positive reinforcement through encouragement notes can serve as a beacon of hope, reminding couples of the potential for positive change and improvement in their relationship dynamics.

Motivation is like a flame that needs constant nurturing to burn brightly. In relationship therapy, this flame can flicker due to setbacks or challenges. Encouragement acts as fuel, reigniting determination and perseverance in the face of adversity. It provides couples with the emotional support needed to weather storms together and emerge stronger on the other side.

Consistent encouragement fosters a supportive reading environment where couples feel validated and understood in their efforts to improve their relationship. These notes serve as gentle reminders of progress made, no matter how small, reinforcing the idea that every step forward counts. By acknowledging each other's efforts and growth, couples can cultivate a sense of mutual appreciation and respect.

In therapy, it is essential to recognize that change is a gradual process that requires patience and dedication. Encouragement notes play a vital role in sustaining motivation, especially during challenging times when doubts may arise. They serve as tangible evidence of hope, reminding couples of the positive outcomes that await them if they continue to invest in their relationship.

By embracing encouragement as a cornerstone of therapy, couples can create a nurturing environment where growth and transformation are not only possible but inevitable. These notes act as beacons of light in moments of darkness, guiding couples toward a brighter future filled with love, understanding, and connection. Through consistent reinforcement and support, couples can navigate the ups and downs of therapy with resilience and optimism.

Implementing Encouragement Notes

Encouragement notes are powerful tools for creating a positive and supportive reading environment for couples seeking to improve their relationships. These notes remind readers of the progress made and the potential for further growth, instilling hope and motivation in them. By incorporating encouragement notes throughout the book, you actively foster a sense of optimism and resilience in your journey towards a stronger relationship. These notes are not mere words on a page but rather small doses of positivity that can uplift spirits and reinforce the importance of perseverance in therapy.

When faced with challenges or setbacks, turning to these encouragement notes can boost morale. They serve as beacons of light during moments of doubt, reminding readers of their capacity for change and improvement. By strategically utilizing encouragement notes, you create a supportive ecosystem within the book that nurtures hope and determination. The consistent presence of these notes emphasizes the belief in the transformative power of therapy and reinforces the idea that positive change is achievable with dedication and effort.

Encouragement notes also help maintain focus on the end goal of relationship improvement, serving as gentle nudges towards continued engagement with therapeutic techniques and exercises. They act as gentle reminders of the rewards that await those who persist through challenges. By integrating these notes into your reading experience, you are setting yourself up for success by cultivating a mindset open to growth and change.

The language used in encouragement notes is crucial, as it should be empathetic, understanding, and empowering. Words can uplift spirits and inspire action, so crafting these notes with care and intention can significantly impact how readers receive them. By infusing each note with compassion and support, you create a safe space within the book where readers feel validated and encouraged to continue their journey toward relationship revitalization.

Incorporating encouragement notes is not just about sprinkling positivity throughout the text; it is about actively engaging with your progress and celebrating small victories. These notes serve as checkpoints that mark your growth and development, reinforcing that every step forward, no matter how small, is significant in the grand scheme of relationship enhancement. Embrace these notes as tokens of self-encouragement and use them as tools to propel yourself towards a more fulfilling partnership.

Remember, the power of encouragement lies in its ability to uplift, inspire, and motivate. By embracing these notes wholeheartedly, you create a more hopeful reading environment and cultivate a mindset primed for positive change. Allow yourself to be guided by these messages of support, knowing that each brings you closer to the relationship you aspire to have.

Maintaining an optimistic relationship outlook is crucial for fostering growth and positive change. It's essential to believe in the potential for improvement and remain committed to revitalizing your connection. Staying hopeful and open-minded creates space for transformation and progress within your relationship. Embracing a positive mindset can be a powerful tool in navigating challenges and setbacks, allowing you to approach issues with resilience and determination.

Remain steadfast in your belief that positive change is possible. Acknowledge the progress you've already made, no matter how small, as it serves as a reminder of your capacity for growth. Celebrate each step forward, reinforcing that improvement is achievable through consistent effort and dedication. Visualize the relationship you aspire to have, focusing on the positive aspects you wish to cultivate.

Stay committed to the process, understanding that transformation takes time and patience. Be gentle with yourself and your partner as you navigate challenges together. Communicate your goals and aspirations openly, fostering a shared vision and mutual support. Encourage each other along the way, offering affirmation and appreciation to bolster morale and strengthen your bond.

Practice gratitude for the moments of connection and growth you experience together. Reflect on the progress you've made as a couple, recognizing the efforts you've both put in towards building a healthier relationship. Express your appreciation for each other's contributions, reinforcing a sense of teamwork and collaboration.

Look for the future optimistically, knowing that continued effort and dedication can lead to profound transformation. Believe in the potential for positive change, both individually and as a couple, envisioning a relationship filled with love, understanding, and mutual respect. Embrace the journey ahead with hope and determination, confident in your ability to create a fulfilling and harmonious partnership.

As we wrap up this discussion, it's crucial to recognize the power of encouragement in the journey of relationship therapy. Motivation is not a constant; it bases and flows, often influenced by the challenges we face and the progress we perceive. This is where encouragement notes are vital tools to reinforce positivity and hope during doubt or stagnation.

Encouragement notes are more than simple affirmations; they are reminders of the capacity each couple has to evolve and improve. Integrating these notes into your daily life creates an environment that nurtures growth and fosters resilience. Imagine opening a note reminding you of your partner's appreciation or highlighting a small victory in your relationship journey. These tokens of motivation can significantly uplift spirits and renew commitment to the therapeutic process.

Moreover, maintaining an optimistic outlook is essential. It's easy to become disheartened when changes don't occur as quickly or visibly as hoped. However, an optimistic perspective helps recognize that each small step forward is a piece of a larger puzzle of improvement. This belief in positive change is beneficial and crucial for sustained effort and ultimate success in therapy.

Let's take control and actively engage with these strategies. Start by writing your first encouragement note today, perhaps noting something you value about your partner or a recent positive interaction. Place these notes where they can be easily found, and let them serve as continual prompts for your progress, no matter how incremental it may seem.

By embracing these practices, not only do we enhance our therapeutic journey, but we also contribute to a stronger, more resilient relationship. Each step forward, guided by encouragement and an optimistic outlook, is a step toward a more connected and fulfilling partnership. Let these tools empower you to navigate your therapy with hope and confidence.

Chapter 13: Celebrating Differences: Culturally Enriched Relationships

"Love doesn't just sit there like a stone; it has

to be made, like bread, remade

all the time, made new."

Ursula K. Le Guin

Embrace the Unfamiliar: How Cultural Differences Can Strengthen Your Bond

In a more connected world than ever, intimate relationships often become the meeting point of diverse cultural backgrounds. Understanding and embracing these differences is not just a necessity but a significant opportunity to deepen and enrich your connection with your partner. This chapter focuses on the essential skills needed to navigate and honor these cultural nuances, which can transform potential conflicts into profound respect and mutual growth.

Cultural diversity in relationships offers a rich tapestry of perspectives that, when understood, can foster a deeper empathy between partners. It requires both individuals to learn about each other's backgrounds actively. This learning process goes beyond mere tolerance—it's about building a foundation of **mutual respect** and understanding that celebrates these differences as strengths rather than hurdles.

The first step is recognizing that misunderstandings stemming from cultural differences are natural. Instead of allowing these moments to create distance, see them as opportunities for both partners to express curiosity and kindness. Doing so sets the stage for open dialogue—a key component in any thriving relationship. Here, we'll explore effective communication strategies that help clarify misunderstandings without assigning blame or fostering resentment.

Building on communication, we delve into practical ways to integrate cultural awareness into everyday interactions within your relationship. Whether it's through food, holidays, language, or rituals, incorporating elements from each partner's background can be an enriching experience that strengthens the bond. This integration helps create an *inclusive environment* where both partners feel valued and understood.

Moreover, fostering an accepting and inclusive atmosphere is crucial for a healthy relationship dynamic. It involves more than just understanding each other's cultures; it requires active participation and willingness to adapt practices inclusive of both partners' backgrounds. Here, actionable advice will be provided to help couples create a space where cultural differences are not just acknowledged but celebrated.

Finally, this chapter emphasizes the importance of continual learning and flexibility in culturally mixed relationships. The journey of cultural exploration is ongoing—it doesn't stop after learning about each other's major holidays or languages. It's about embracing new aspects of your partner's culture as they naturally unfold within the context of your relationship.

Couples can navigate their differences more effectively by focusing on these areas and building a stronger, more resilient union that honors both partners' unique backgrounds. The goal is clear: cultivate a relationship where cultural diversity is seen as an asset that enriches your connection rather than a barrier to overcome.

Cultural differences can add depth and richness to relationships but present challenges if not cared for. Navigating and honoring these differences within intimate relationships is crucial for fostering understanding and mutual respect. Recognizing that each partner brings their unique cultural background, beliefs, and practices into the relationship, shaping their perspectives and behaviors is essential.

Communication is key when it comes to navigating cultural

differences. Encouraging open dialogue about each other's cultural backgrounds, traditions, and values can lead to a deeper understanding of each partner's origin. Active listening plays a significant role in this process, allowing partners to truly hear and acknowledge each other's experiences without judgment or assumptions.

Respecting each other's cultural differences involves validation and acceptance. It's essential to recognize that what may seem normal or acceptable in one culture might be perceived differently in another. Empathy plays a crucial role here, allowing partners to step into each other's shoes and see the world through their eyes.

Setting boundaries and establishing clear communication channels can help navigate cultural differences effectively. Partners should openly discuss their comfort levels with certain cultural practices or traditions and find common ground on approaching potential conflicts due to these differences. Mutual compromise and flexibility are essential for creating a harmonious balance in the relationship while honoring each other's cultural identities.

Practical Steps for Building Mutual Respect and Understanding

Building mutual respect and understanding through cultural awareness is essential in fostering healthy and enriching relationships. Cultural differences can be a source of strength or a point of contention in relationships, depending on how they are approached. Embracing cultural diversity within a relationship can lead to deeper connections and a broader perspective on the world. Acknowledging that each individual brings their unique background, beliefs, and traditions into the relationship, shaping their worldview and values is crucial.

Partners must engage in open and honest conversations about their cultural backgrounds to build mutual respect and understanding. Active listening plays a significant role in this process, allowing each partner to share their experiences without judgment. Empathy is key in these discussions, as it helps partners understand each other's perspectives and feelings more deeply. By showing empathy toward your partner's cultural differences, you validate their experiences and foster a sense of acceptance within the relationship.

Cultural awareness involves educating oneself about different traditions, customs, and values. Taking the time to learn about your partner's culture demonstrates respect and interest in their background. Engaging in cultural activities can also strengthen your bond as you explore new experiences and traditions as a couple. You support and appreciate your partner's heritage by actively participating in each other's cultural practices.

Challenges may arise when cultural differences clash, leading to misunderstandings or conflicts within the relationship. It is important to address these challenges with patience and understanding, seeking common ground while respecting each other's perspectives. Conflict resolution skills are crucial in navigating cultural differences, allowing partners to communicate effectively and find mutually beneficial solutions.

Fostering inclusivity and acceptance within the relationship involves celebrating each other's uniqueness while embracing diversity. Creating a safe space for open dialogue about cultural differences encourages growth and mutual understanding between partners. By valuing and respecting each other's cultures, you strengthen the foundation of your relationship, promoting harmony and unity despite any differences that may arise.

In conclusion, building mutual respect and understanding through cultural awareness is a continuous process that requires effort from both partners. Embracing diversity within the relationship enriches the bond between partners, fostering a sense of connection that transcends cultural barriers. By actively engaging with each other's backgrounds, beliefs, and traditions, couples can create a more inclusive and accepting environment that celebrates their differences.

Cultivating an inclusive and accepting environment within a relationship is essential for fostering deeper connections and enriching relational dynamics. By embracing and celebrating differences, couples can create a space where each partner feels respected, valued, and understood. Mutual respect is the cornerstone of a healthy relationship, and acknowledging and honoring each other's cultural backgrounds is a significant step toward building that respect.

Communication plays a vital role in creating an inclusive environment. Encouraging open and honest dialogue about cultural differences can help bridge any gaps in understanding.

Active listening is key; it allows partners to hear each other's perspectives without judgment. Empathy also plays a crucial role in fostering inclusivity, enabling partners to step into each other's shoes and see the world from their perspective.

Education is another powerful tool in building an inclusive relationship. Taking the time to learn about your partner's culture, traditions, and beliefs shows that you value their background and are willing to invest in understanding them better. Celebrating important cultural holidays or traditions together can also strengthen the bond between partners and create shared memories that honor both backgrounds.

Resolving conflicts through a lens of cultural understanding can prevent misunderstandings from escalating. When disagreements arise, taking a step back to consider how cultural differences may influence the situation can lead to more productive conversations. Seeking compromise while respecting each other's cultural values can help find common ground without dismissing either partner's background.

Creating an accepting environment means embracing diversity within the relationship. It involves recognizing that differences enrich the partnership rather than divide it. By valuing each other's unique perspectives and experiences, couples can create a space where both partners feel seen, heard, and appreciated for who they are.

Inclusive relationships are not devoid of challenges, but they are built on a foundation of respect, empathy, communication, and cultural awareness. Embracing these principles fosters a sense of unity while still honoring individual identities within the partnership. By fostering an inclusive and accepting environment, couples can navigate cultural differences gracefully, creating a stronger bond based on mutual understanding and respect.

Recognizing and respecting cultural differences is not just a necessity but a profound opportunity to deepen the connection in your relationship. Through this chapter, we've explored practical strategies to navigate these differences effectively, ensuring that both partners feel valued and understood. By building on the foundation of mutual respect and cultural awareness, relationships can transform into a rich tapestry of shared experiences and perspectives, enhancing the intimacy and strength of the bond.

Navigating cultural nuances within your relationship requires patience and commitment. Engaging in open and honest dialogues without assumptions or judgments is important. These conversations are stepping stones to gaining deeper insights into each other's worldviews and values. Remember, every step taken towards understanding is a step towards a more harmonious partnership.

Building mutual respect is more than acknowledging differences; it's about actively celebrating them. This involves listening to understand and participating in each other's cultural practices when appropriate. Such participation shows respect and enriches your life experiences, bringing a new level of depth to your relationship.

Fostering an inclusive environment is crucial. It's about creating a space where both partners can freely express their cultural identities without fear of dismissal or ridicule. This inclusivity strengthens trust and solidarity between partners, making the relationship a haven for both individuals to thrive.

Take action today. Discuss what you've learned with your partner and explore ways to incorporate this new understanding into your daily interactions. Simple gestures of acknowledgment and appreciation of each other's cultural backgrounds can make a significant difference.

By embracing these practices, you and your partner will easily navigate cultural differences and build a stronger, more resilient relationship. As you apply these principles, remember that the journey of cultural exploration and mutual respect is ongoing and always ripe with opportunities for growth and deeper connection. Embrace it with an open heart and mind, ready to learn and grow together.

Chapter 14: Ounce of Prevention: Therapy as Relationship Maintenance

"We loved with a love that was more than love."

Edgar Allan Poe

Is Waiting for a Crisis the Only Time for Couples Therapy?

In the landscape of modern relationships, the notion of couples therapy often conjures images of last-ditch efforts to save a crumbling partnership. However, this chapter challenges that reactive mindset and introduces a more proactive approach to using therapy as an integral part of maintaining a healthy relationship. By viewing therapy as routine maintenance rather than an emergency repair, couples can foster a relationship that survives and thrives.

Therapy as preventative care is not just a novel idea; it's a transformative one. It shifts the perception from therapy being the "last resort" to it being a "regular tune-up." This chapter explores how engaging in therapy before problems become crises can strengthen the bonds between partners, ensuring that minor issues don't become insurmountable challenges. The goal is to equip couples with tools for ongoing communication improvement, conflict resolution, and deepening intimacy—all foundational elements discussed throughout this book.

Embracing Proactivity in Relationships

Adopting proactive strategies in therapy can significantly alter relationship dynamics for the better. This isn't about fixing something broken but nurturing what's already there to prevent breakage. We'll explore how regular therapeutic sessions can serve as a diagnostic and preventive tool, helping partners understand and manage their evolving needs and expectations.

Moreover, this chapter underscores the long-term benefits of consistent therapeutic engagement. Regular check-ins with a therapist aren't just helpful; they're crucial for the health of a relationship in the same way that regular doctor visits are crucial for physical health. These sessions provide a safe space to address concerns before they escalate and reinforce positive patterns of interaction.

Sustaining Connection Through Therapy

The emphasis on regular therapeutic involvement aligns with our broader discussion on effective communication and intimacy-building techniques introduced earlier in the book. Here, we tie these threads together, showing how sustained therapeutic engagement resolves conflicts and sparks ongoing personal growth and mutual understanding within a couple.

This proactive approach is grounded in practicality and tailored to fit real-world relationships. It strips away the complexity often associated with counseling and focuses on straightforward, actionable strategies that couples can apply immediately. By demystifying the process and highlighting its accessibility, we encourage couples to take control of their relationship's health through informed action.

As we conclude our exploration in subsequent chapters, remember that the journey toward a revitalized connection does not end here. The principles and practices in this guide are designed to be revisited and adapted as your relationship grows and changes over time. Regularly engaging in couples therapy is about avoiding pitfalls and reaching new heights together.

By redefining couples therapy as an essential aspect of relationship upkeep rather than an emergency measure, we empower couples to nurture their bond proactively. This shift in perspective is crucial for any couple committed to sustaining a vibrant, healthy partnership over time.

Couples therapy is not just for resolving conflicts but also a powerful tool for preventing them. By proactively engaging in therapy, couples can address underlying issues before they escalate, fostering a healthier and more resilient relationship. Viewing therapy as a form of relationship maintenance rather than a last resort can transform how couples approach their partnership. Preventive therapy helps identify potential sources of tension, improve communication skills, and strengthen emotional bonds.

Regular sessions with a therapist can serve as check-ins for the relationship, allowing couples to address small concerns before they snowball into significant problems. It provides a safe space for open and honest communication, which is essential for maintaining trust and intimacy. Therapy sessions offer an opportunity to explore individual triggers and patterns that may impact the relationship, enabling couples to make proactive changes to better their partnership.

Proactive engagement in therapy can help couples develop a deeper understanding of each other. By delving into past experiences, beliefs, and behaviors, couples can gain insights into the root causes of their conflicts. This understanding paves the way for empathy and compassion, which are essential to a strong and lasting relationship. Therapy is a preventive measure that equips couples with the tools to navigate challenges effectively.

In addition to addressing current issues, preventive therapy builds resilience within the relationship. Couples learn to adapt to changes, handle stressors, and communicate effectively, even in challenging situations. This proactive approach not only prevents future conflicts but also strengthens the foundation of the partnership, making it more durable and fulfilling. Therapy is a proactive investment in the health and longevity of the relationship.

Proactive Strategies For Issue Resolution and Dynamics Improvement.

In maintaining a healthy relationship, proactive strategies are crucial in issue resolution and dynamic improvement. Rather than waiting for problems to escalate, taking preventive measures can help address issues before they become significant hurdles. One effective strategy is regular communication, where partners openly discuss their feelings, concerns, and needs. By fostering an environment of transparency and honesty, couples can prevent misunderstandings and build trust.

Another proactive approach involves setting boundaries and expectations. Clear boundaries help establish respect and understanding between partners, reducing conflicts arising from crossed lines. Individuals can constructively navigate disagreements when they know each other's limits and preferences.

Implementing problem-solving techniques can also be beneficial.

Instead of letting issues linger unresolved, couples can tackle them head-on using structured methods. This could include active listening, compromise, and finding mutually agreeable solutions. By addressing challenges promptly, couples can prevent small disagreements from snowballing into larger problems.

Regular self-reflection is a key proactive strategy for maintaining a healthy relationship. Each partner should take the time to assess their thoughts, feelings, and behaviors. By identifying areas for personal growth and improvement, individuals can contribute positively to the partnership.

Emphasizing Mutual Growth

Prioritizing mutual growth within the relationship is another crucial proactive strategy. Couples should support each other's aspirations, goals, and personal development. By encouraging individual growth within the partnership, couples can strengthen their bond and create a supportive environment for each other's success.

Seeking Professional Guidance

In some cases, seeking professional guidance proactively can be immensely beneficial. Couples therapy doesn't have to be reserved for crises; it can serve as a preventive measure to address underlying issues before they escalate. Therapists provide tools and techniques to improve communication, resolve conflicts, and strengthen the emotional connection between partners.

Cultivating Gratitude

Practicing gratitude regularly is a simple yet powerful proactive strategy for maintaining a healthy relationship. Expressing appreciation for each other's efforts, qualities, and presence fosters a positive atmosphere within the partnership. By acknowledging the good in each other consistently, couples can reinforce their bond and weather challenges more effectively.

Epilogue

"The more love you give away, the more you will have."

Unknown

Embracing a Future of Deeper Connection and Understanding

As we draw this journey to a close, I hope the paths in these pages serve as guides and gateways to a renewed sense of partnership and love in your relationship. You've been equipped with tools and insights designed to break down barriers of miscommunication, reignite intimacy, and foster a deeper connection with your partner.

The principles and techniques discussed are more than theoretical concepts; they are practical tools tailored for real-world application. Every conversation you engage in, every conflict you navigate, and every moment of shared vulnerability is an opportunity to apply these strategies. By integrating these practices into your daily interactions, you'll see improvements in your relationship and feel more empowered and confident in your ability to manage and resolve conflicts.

To recap the cornerstone elements, effective communication is the bedrock of a thriving relationship. We explored how active listening, empathy expression, and clear articulation of needs can transform how partners interact. Conflict resolution was demystified, presenting it not as a battle to be won but as a collaborative process to find solutions that respect both partners' perspectives. Lastly, we delved into ways to enhance intimacy—physically, emotionally, and intellectually- creating a well-rounded bond that can withstand the tests of time.

Now, it's time to put these insights into action. Start small if you need to, perhaps by dedicating time each day to talk openly about your thoughts and feelings or by planning regular date nights to reconnect and create new memories. Remember, the goal is not perfection but progress.

While this book aims to cover comprehensively the aspects of couples therapy techniques for enhancing relationships, it is important to acknowledge its limitations. Individual differences in relationships mean that some strategies may need adaptation. Furthermore, some deeply entrenched issues might require professional intervention beyond self-help methods.

I encourage you not only to read and reflect but also to act. Harness the power of communication to create change within your relationship. Let every day be an opportunity for growth and every challenge a stepping stone towards deeper understanding.

As you continue on this path, remember that change is a journey, not a destination. It requires patience, commitment, and, above all, love.

Let us part with these words by Vincent Van Gogh:

"The heart of man is very much like the sea,

it has its storms, it has its tides,

and in its depths, it has

its pearls, too."

May you find your pearls as you navigate the depths of your relationship together.

Conclusion

"Where there is love, there is life."

Mahatma Gandhi

As you reach the end of this book, take a moment to reflect on the journey you've embarked upon. The insights, strategies, and exercises presented within these pages are designed to serve as a roadmap for fostering a healthier, more resilient relationship. By now, you should be equipped with a deeper understanding of effective communication techniques, conflict resolution methodologies, and ways to enhance intimacy. Each of these elements plays a crucial role in building a strong foundation upon which your partnership can thrive.

Maintaining a healthy relationship is an ongoing process that requires continuous effort and dedication from both partners. It's essential to regularly revisit the principles and practices outlined in this guide, integrating them into your daily interactions. This helps address immediate concerns and prevents potential issues from escalating. Consistency is key: practice open dialogue, empathy, and active listening to ensure your relationship remains robust.

While the journey toward a revitalized relationship may be challenging, it's also incredibly rewarding. The tools you've gained here are versatile and adaptable, capable of addressing various issues, from minor misunderstandings to significant conflicts. By approaching each challenge with a solutions-oriented mindset, you create an environment where both partners feel heard, respected, and valued. Remember that conflict is not inherently negative; it's an opportunity for growth and deeper understanding when addressed constructively.

Consider incorporating regular relationship check-ins further to reinforce the bond between you and your partner. These can be formal or informal, but the key is to create a safe space for both partners to express their thoughts, feelings, and needs. By doing so, you can proactively address any concerns and celebrate successes together, reinforcing your commitment to each other.

In addition to regular check-ins, shared experiences play a vital role in maintaining intimacy. Whether through hobbies, travel, or simply spending quality time together, shared activities help to strengthen your emotional and intellectual connection. Being vulnerable and open with each other during these times can deepen your bond, making your relationship more resilient to external pressures.

It's important to acknowledge that every relationship is unique, and each couple's journey toward a stronger connection may look different. While this book offers a comprehensive set of tools and strategies, it's crucial to tailor these to your circumstances. Flexibility and adaptability are essential as you navigate the complexities of your relationship. Don't hesitate to seek professional help; sometimes, an external perspective can provide invaluable guidance.

As you apply the principles discussed in this book, remember that progress often comes in small, incremental steps rather than giant leaps. Celebrate the small victories along the way and remain patient with each other. The ultimate goal is not perfection but growth and understanding. By consistently investing time and effort into your relationship, you can build a sustainable, loving partnership that stands the test of time.

In conclusion, consider these key takeaways as you move forward:

- **Communication**: Practice active listening and express your needs clearly.
- **Conflict Resolution**: Approach disagreements with a solutions-oriented mindset.
- **Intimacy**: Cultivate emotional, intellectual, and physical connection.
- **Consistency**: Make ongoing relationship maintenance a priority.
- **Adaptability**: Tailor strategies to fit your unique relationship dynamics.
- **Professional Support**: Seek professional counseling when needed.

May these principles guide you toward a deeper, more meaningful connection with your partner. Your journey together is an ongoing growth, understanding, and love process. Embrace each moment, and cherish the path you are on together.

Bonus Material

Your Questions, Answered!

1. How can we balance relationship maintenance with our busy work schedules?

Balancing relationship maintenance with busy work schedules can be challenging, but it is achievable with thoughtful planning and intentional effort. Time management forms the cornerstone of this balance. Start by identifying pockets of time where both partners are free. No matter how brief, these moments can be effectively used for meaningful interactions. For instance, you could consider having a breakfast date at the beginning of the week or setting aside time in the evenings to unwind. The key is to be deliberate about these moments, treating them as important appointments that deserve your full attention.

Moreover, leveraging technology can also play a significant role in keeping the connection strong despite hectic schedules. Regular text messages, video calls, or short, heartfelt emails can be reminders of your commitment to each other. It's the small, consistent gestures that often make a big difference. Scheduled video calls during lunch breaks or at the end of the day can provide a venue for catching up and sharing experiences.

Communication doesn't always require long, uninterrupted time; rather, it's the quality and consistency that counts.

Another strategy is to integrate relationship maintenance into your daily routines. This could be as simple as cooking dinner together, engaging in a shared hobby, or working side by side. By involving each other in these regular activities, you spend time together and create a sense of partnership and shared responsibility. This approach helps incorporate relationship-building into the fabric of daily life, making it less of a task and a natural part of your routine.

Lastly, creating and adhering to boundaries between work and personal life is essential. Designate certain times or areas as 'work-free zones' where the focus is solely on each other. Ensure that when you are together, distractions are minimized—turn off work notifications and resist the urge to discuss work-related stress. This dedicated quality time can help to strengthen your bond and make both partners feel valued and prioritized. Remember, a balanced approach, where both work and relationship needs are addressed, fosters a more supportive and harmonious partnership.

2. What are some effective strategies for rekindling intimacy after emotional distance?

Rekindling intimacy after a period of emotional distance can seem daunting, but several effective strategies can help rebuild that connection. The first step is to acknowledge and address the underlying issues that may have led to the emotional distance. Open, honest communication is essential. Both partners must feel safe expressing their thoughts and feelings without fear of judgment or retaliation. This can be facilitated through structured conversation techniques, such as active listening and reflective responses, ensuring each partner feels heard and understood.

Practicing empathy is crucial in this process. Understanding and validating each other's emotions can provide a stronger foundation for reconnection. It is also important to recognize that emotional distance often develops gradually, and unraveling it requires patience and persistent effort. Couples may benefit from setting small, achievable goals to rebuild their intimacy gradually. These could include daily check-ins, expressing appreciation regularly, or engaging in new activities to spark joy and curiosity about each other once more.

Physical touch is another powerful tool in rekindling intimacy. Simple gestures such as holding hands, hugging, or even sitting close to one another can help rebuild a physical connection, enhancing emotional closeness. Incorporating rituals of affection into your daily routine can convey warmth and safety. Couples may also consider scheduling regular date nights where they can focus solely on each other without the distractions of everyday life. These dedicated times can allow them to explore each other's interests, dreams, and experiences, helping refresh and renew their bond.

Lastly, seeking professional support can be incredibly beneficial. A trained therapist can offer guided techniques and neutral perspectives that can aid in navigating the complexity of rebuilding intimacy. Therapy provides a structured environment where both partners can explore their feelings in-depth, learn new communication methods, and develop effective coping strategies for future conflicts. Investing in professional guidance shows a commitment to the relationship and provides valuable tools for sustaining intimacy in the long term. Couples can successfully rekindle their intimacy and strengthen their emotional connection with perseverance, empathy, and supportive strategies.

3. How do we address conflicts when one partner tends to avoid confrontation?

Addressing conflicts when one partner tends to avoid confrontation requires a multi-faceted approach to ensure that issues are resolved effectively while maintaining the emotional well-being of both individuals. Conflict avoidance can stem from various reasons, such as fear of escalation, discomfort with emotional expression, or past negative experiences with conflict. Understanding the root cause of the avoidance is crucial in developing a strategy that accommodates both partners' needs and promotes healthy communication.

The first step in addressing this issue is fostering a safe and supportive environment for open dialogue. The partner who avoids confrontation needs assurance that their feelings and perspectives will be respected and valued. Establishing clear communication norms, such as using "I" statements, avoiding blame, and actively listening, can create a space where both partners feel comfortable expressing their thoughts.

Implementing these practices can reduce the fear of confrontation by emphasizing collaboration and mutual respect rather than conflict.

It's also important to recognize the significance of timing and setting when discussing contentious issues. Finding a neutral, calm environment free from distractions can help reduce stress and facilitate more productive conversations. Avoid initiating discussions when either partner is tired, hungry, or stressed, as these conditions can exacerbate tension and hinder constructive dialogue. Taking the time to choose an appropriate moment can demonstrate consideration and patience, making the conflict resolution process less daunting for the partner who tends to avoid confrontation.

Furthermore, incorporating conflict resolution techniques such as compromise, negotiation, and problem-solving can help balance the dynamics between partners. Encouraging the partner who avoids confrontation to participate in identifying solutions and agreeing on compromises empowers them and fosters a sense of involvement and control. Utilizing these techniques shifts the focus from the conflict to finding mutually beneficial outcomes, reducing anxiety and reluctance to engage in confrontation.

Lastly, seeking the assistance of a professional can be highly beneficial, especially if the pattern of conflict avoidance is deeply ingrained. A trained therapist or counselor can offer valuable insights and tools to help both partners navigate their communication styles and address underlying issues contributing to avoiding confrontation. Therapy can provide a structured environment for exploring feelings, developing coping strategies, and practicing new ways of addressing conflicts. With professional guidance, couples can build stronger, more resilient relationships where both partners feel heard and valued.

4. Can regular relationship check-ins become monotonous, and how can we keep them engaging?

Regular relationship check-ins, while essential to maintaining a healthy and thriving relationship, can sometimes become monotonous if they are not approached with creativity and mindfulness. The routine aspect of these check-ins may induce a sense of predictability that, over time, can diminish the excitement and engagement that partners experience during these sessions. However, several strategies can be employed to keep relationship check-ins engaging and meaningful, ensuring they continue serving their purpose effectively.

One effective approach is to vary the format and location of the check-ins. Instead of always sitting at the dining table or couch, couples can choose different settings that evoke a different mood and presence. For instance, conducting a check-in during a walk in the park, over a picnic, or even while doing a shared activity like cooking together can bring a fresh perspective to the conversation. Changing the scenery can break the routine and add an element of spontaneity, making the process feel less like a chore and more like an enjoyable time spent together.

Another strategy to keep check-ins engaging is incorporating playful and creative elements. Couples can use prompts or conversation starters that delve into fun and varied topics, such as discussing their dream vacations, sharing fond memories, or even planning hypothetical scenarios together. This approach makes the check-ins more enjoyable and allows couples to explore different facets of each other's personalities and imaginations, fostering deeper connections and understanding.

Additionally, focusing on positive reinforcement and celebrations can greatly enhance the engagement level of relationship check-ins. Partners can take turns expressing appreciation for each other's efforts and acknowledging their progress, however small it may be. Setting small goals and celebrating their achievement can infuse the check-ins with a sense of accomplishment and motivation. This positive reinforcement creates an environment of support and encouragement, making both partners look forward to the next check-in rather than viewing it as a routine task.

Lastly, it is essential to maintain open and honest communication about the check-in process itself. Partners should feel free to discuss what aspects of the check-ins they find valuable and what areas may need adjustments. Regularly seeking feedback and being willing to adapt the process as necessary ensures that the check-ins remain relevant and beneficial. Engaging in a meta-conversation about how to make the check-ins more meaningful can be a potent way of keeping the dialogue fresh and engaging.

Couples can transform regular relationship check-ins from a monotonous routine into a dynamic and enriching practice by incorporating variety, creativity, positive reinforcement, and open communication. This approach helps maintain the vitality and emotional connection crucial for a lasting and fulfilling relationship.

5. How can we maintain a healthy relationship when dealing with long-distance or irregular time together?

Maintaining a healthy relationship when dealing with long-distance or irregular time together can be quite challenging, but it's certainly achievable with effort and commitment from both partners. One of the key components to making this work is consistent and effective communication. Without physical presence, communication becomes the primary mode of maintaining a connection. This means exchanging routine updates, engaging in meaningful conversations, and discussing each other's feelings, dreams, and concerns. Technology plays a significant role here, offering myriad ways to stay connected through video calls, messaging apps, or even traditional emails and letters. Regular check-ins at an agreed-upon schedule can help create a sense of normalcy and reliability, ensuring both partners feel supported and valued.

Another crucial aspect is setting clear expectations and boundaries. Long-distance relationships often come with uncertainties and misunderstandings if expectations are not laid out. It's important for both partners to discuss their needs, the amount of contact they expect, and how they plan to handle issues like jealousy or loneliness. Setting these boundaries can create a secure emotional framework where individuals know where they stand and how to navigate potential challenges. Creating a "relationship contract" that includes these elements can be practical, giving both partners a concrete reference point.

Trust is also paramount in sustaining a long-distance relationship. This relationship tests trust in various ways, especially when partners contend with time zone differences and limited physical interaction. Building and maintaining trust involves honesty and transparency about one's activities and feelings. It also means giving your partner the benefit of the doubt and not allowing insecurities to drive your interactions. Trust can be nurtured through actions that demonstrate commitment, such as planning future visits or setting long-term goals to work toward the time when distance is no longer a barrier.

Lastly, keep the romance alive by finding creative ways to show love and appreciation. Small gestures like sending care packages, love letters, or surprise gifts can significantly uplift your partner's spirits. Virtual date nights can also help create a shared experience, whether watching a movie together, cooking the same meal, or even playing games online. Celebrating milestones and creating new traditions, even from a distance, helps to strengthen the emotional bond and provides shared experiences that both partners can look back on fondly. By embracing these strategies, couples can survive the challenges of long-distance or irregular time together and thrive and grow stronger through the experience.

6. What are some signs that we might need professional support or counseling?

Recognizing when a relationship might benefit from professional support or counseling is a crucial step in maintaining its health and longevity. One significant indicator is persistent unresolved conflict. If couples find themselves in a cycle of frequent arguments or disagreements that never reach a resolution, it may be time to seek a neutral third party. These recurring conflicts can create an environment of tension and resentment, significantly affecting the emotional well-being of both partners. A trained therapist or counselor can provide strategies and tools to break these patterns, facilitating more effective communication and conflict resolution.

Another key sign is a lack of intimacy or emotional connection. When partners feel emotionally distant or notice a decline in physical intimacy, it can signify deeper issues that require attention. This emotional gap may manifest as one or both partners withdrawing, spending less time together, or lacking interest in each other's lives. Professional support can help identify the root causes of this disconnection, offering ways to rebuild trust and intimacy. Through counseling, couples can explore their feelings in a safe space, helping to rekindle the closeness fundamental to a healthy relationship.

Feelings of being stuck or stagnant in the relationship also signal the need for professional intervention. When one or both partners feel trapped, unable to move forward or see the growth potential, it can lead to frustration and dissatisfaction. This feeling of stagnation can arise from various issues, including unmet needs, unspoken grievances, or life changes that have not been adequately addressed. Counseling can provide a structured environment for addressing these concerns, helping couples to set achievable goals and work towards a more fulfilling and dynamic relationship.

Experiencing significant life transitions or stressors is another situation where professional support can be invaluable. Life events such as job loss, moving to a new city, health issues, or becoming parents can place immense pressure on a relationship. These stressors can expose cracks in the relationship that were previously manageable or create new challenges that couples are ill-equipped to handle on their own. A professional can offer coping mechanisms and facilitate discussions that allow both partners to navigate these changes together, strengthening their bond.

In summary, paying attention to unresolved conflicts, emotional disconnection, feelings of stagnation, and significant life stressors can help couples identify when to seek professional support. Engaging in counseling is not a sign of failure; instead, it is a proactive step towards a healthier and more satisfying relationship.

7. Are specific activities or hobbies particularly good for strengthening a relationship?

Engaging in specific activities or hobbies can significantly strengthen relationships by fostering bonding, communication, and a sense of shared achievement. One of the primary benefits of shared activities is that they provide couples with opportunities to spend quality time together. This shared time allows partners to connect deeper, beyond the daily routines and responsibilities that can often create emotional distance. For instance, taking up a hobby like cooking together can turn everyday meals into an enjoyable, collaborative experience where both partners contribute and create something meaningful.

In addition to spending quality time, engaging in shared activities enhances communication. Participating in hobbies that require teamwork and coordination, such as playing a sport, gardening, or even undertaking home improvement projects, necessitates dialogue and collaboration. These activities can help couples hone their communication skills, express their thoughts, listen actively, and work through challenges together. Improved communication fosters mutual understanding and respect, which is essential to a healthy and resilient relationship.

Furthermore, hobbies can bring a sense of novelty and excitement into a relationship. Trying new activities together, like dance classes, hiking, or traveling to new destinations, can keep the relationship vibrant and dynamic. The excitement of learning something new or exploring new places together introduces an element of surprise and adventure, helping to stave off monotony. This sense of shared discovery becomes a reservoir of positive memories that couples can look back on, reinforcing their bond.

Finally, shared activities can foster personal growth and mutual support. When partners engage in hobbies they are passionate about, they develop their individual skills and interests and support each other's growth. This support can be incredibly validating and empowering, demonstrating a genuine interest in each other's happiness and personal development. Couples reinforce their emotional connection and build a solid foundation of mutual respect and admiration by celebrating each other's progress and achievements.

In summary, specific activities and hobbies can be crucial in strengthening a relationship by providing opportunities for quality time, enhancing communication, introducing excitement, and encouraging mutual growth. Through these shared experiences, couples can deepen their connection, making their relationship more fulfilling and resilient.

8. How do we navigate and resolve differences in our relationship goals and aspirations?

Navigating and resolving differences in relationship goals and aspirations requires open communication, compromise, and mutual respect. It's natural for partners to have individual aspirations that may not always align perfectly, and addressing these differences thoughtfully is crucial for the relationship's health. The first step is to create a safe and non-judgmental space for both partners to express their dreams and goals. It's important that each person feels heard and valued, even if their aspirations differ. Setting aside regular times to discuss these topics can ensure that both partners are on the same page and can revisit their goals as they evolve.

Once both individuals have articulated their goals, finding common ground is the next critical step. This involves identifying areas where aspirations overlap and brainstorming ways to achieve mutual satisfaction. Sometimes goals may seem mutually exclusive at first glance, but through creative problem-solving and a willingness to bend, couples often find ways to integrate both sets of aspirations. For instance, one partner may wish to travel extensively, while the other aims to advance in their career. A possible compromise could involve taking shorter, more frequent trips that allow the traveling partner to fulfill their wanderlust without significantly impeding the other's career progression.

Managing expectations and defining what constitutes a fair compromise is vital. This doesn't mean one partner always capitulates to the other's wishes, but both are willing to make concessions to support each other's happiness. Transparency in communication is key here; setting clear boundaries and discussing potential conflicts upfront can prevent resentment from building up. Additionally, being realistic about what each partner can reasonably accomplish within the relationship framework helps set attainable goals.

Lastly, ongoing adaptability and flexibility are essential as life circumstances change. Goals and aspirations are dynamic and can shift due to age, career changes, or family responsibilities. Continuous dialogue about these changes ensures that both partners remain aligned and can adjust their plans accordingly. Continuous relationship check-ins can reaffirm both partners' commitment to supporting each other's evolving aspirations, thus maintaining a balanced and fulfilling partnership. Couples can navigate their differences with understanding and grace through these strategies, creating a supportive and harmonious relationship.

9. What practical steps can we take to ensure active listening becomes a habit in our relationship?

Active listening is a fundamental skill that can significantly enhance the quality of a relationship by fostering a deeper understanding and emotional connection between partners. To make active listening a habit, couples can take several practical steps. First and foremost, setting aside dedicated time for conversations without distractions is crucial. This means turning off electronic devices, minimizing background noise, and ensuring both partners are fully present. This quality time allows each person to feel valued and listened to, creating an environment conducive to meaningful dialogue.

Another practical step is to practice reflective listening. This technique involves paraphrasing what the other person has said and repeating it to them to confirm understanding. For example, if one partner expresses frustration about work, the other might respond, "It sounds like you're feeling stressed about the upcoming deadline." This shows that the listener is paying attention and provides an opportunity to clarify any misunderstandings. Reflective listening can help partners feel heard and understood, reducing the likelihood of miscommunication.

Maintaining eye contact and using non-verbal cues, such as nodding or leaning in slightly, also play a critical role in active listening. These gestures signal attentiveness and genuine interest in what the other person is saying. Additionally, asking open-ended questions can encourage deeper conversation and demonstrate that the listener is invested in understanding the speaker's perspective. Questions like, "How did that make you feel?" or "What do you think we should do next?" invite the speaker to elaborate, providing more insight into their thoughts and emotions.

Lastly, practicing patience and avoiding interrupting while the other person is speaking is essential. Giving each partner the space to express their feelings and thoughts without fear of being cut off fosters a sense of safety and respect. If emotions run high, taking a few moments to breathe and compose oneself before responding can prevent reactive or defensive comments, promoting a more constructive and empathetic exchange. By implementing these practical steps, couples can cultivate a habit of active listening, thereby strengthening their emotional connection and enhancing overall relationship satisfaction.

10.   How can we deal with external pressures, such as family expectations or social influences, that affect our relationship?

Dealing with external pressures, such as family expectations or social influences, is a common challenge that can impact the dynamics of a relationship. These pressures often stem from cultural norms, traditional values, or close family members' and friends' desires and opinions. To address these influences constructively, couples must first acknowledge their existence and understand how they affect their relationship. Open and honest communication between partners is crucial in identifying and discussing the specific external pressures they face. By recognizing these influences, partners can better prepare to manage them collectively.

One practical step in dealing with family expectations is setting clear boundaries. Couples should have candid conversations about their values, goals, and the extent to which they are willing to accommodate family desires. Establishing these boundaries early on helps prevent misunderstandings and conflicts later. For instance, if one partner's family has strong opinions about holiday celebrations or career choices, the couple should discuss navigating these expectations while staying true to their priorities. Communicating these boundaries to family members respectfully yet firmly can help maintain harmony while preserving the couple's autonomy.

Social influences like societal norms and peer pressure can also create challenges. Society often dictates what a successful relationship should look like, from financial achievements to lifestyle choices. Couples must critically evaluate these norms and decide which aspects align with their values and aspirations. This process involves self-reflection and mutual support, allowing partners to build relationships based on their strengths and desires rather than external standards. For example, if societal pressures emphasize career success over quality time together, partners should discuss balancing these demands in a way that works best for them.

Equally important is the need for mutual support and a united front when facing external pressures. Partners must prioritize their relationship and present a cohesive stance to outsiders. This unity demonstrates that their bond is strong and resistant to external stressors. When family members or friends see a couple working together effectively, they are more likely to respect the couple's decisions and boundaries. Regular reassessment of the couple's strategies for dealing with external pressures ensures they remain adaptable and resilient, regardless of their challenges. Through these approaches, couples can successfully navigate the complexities of external pressures, fostering a fulfilling and respectful relationship of their individualities.

11.   What are the best ways to foster emotional vulnerability without feeling exposed or insecure?

Fostering emotional vulnerability in a relationship involves creating an environment where both partners feel safe to express their deepest feelings without fear of judgment or rejection. Emotional vulnerability is crucial for building a strong emotional connection, yet it often feels risky because it requires exposing one's innermost thoughts and emotions. Several strategies can be employed to foster this kind of openness without feeling exposed or insecure.

Firstly, it is essential to establish a foundation of mutual trust and respect. Trust is built over time through consistent actions that demonstrate reliability, honesty, and integrity. When partners trust each other, they are more likely to feel secure in sharing their vulnerabilities. Respecting each other's boundaries is equally critical. This involves acknowledging and honoring each other's emotional limits and being sensitive to cues that indicate discomfort or hesitation. A relationship built on trust and respect provides a secure base for both partners to explore emotional depths.

Creating a safe communication space is another vital step. This means setting aside dedicated time where both partners can talk without interruptions or distractions. During these conversations, the focus should be on active listening and providing empathetic responses. It helps to use "I" statements to communicate personal feelings and experiences, which reduces the likelihood of the other person feeling blamed or attacked. For instance, instead of saying, "You never listen to me," one might say, "I feel unheard when I'm sharing my thoughts." This approach encourages open dialogue and reduces defensiveness.

Encouraging small steps toward vulnerability can also build confidence over time. Sharing low-stakes feelings and gradually moving to more significant emotional disclosures can help partners become more comfortable with vulnerability. Celebrating these moments of openness, no matter how small reinforces the behavior and makes it more likely to continue. Additionally, expressing appreciation and validation when a partner opens up can significantly boost their confidence to share more. Both partners must understand that vulnerability is a process and allow each other the grace and patience to navigate it.

Lastly, it is important to cultivate a non-judgmental attitude within the relationship. Refraining from criticism, ridicule, or invalidation when a partner shares their emotions is paramount. Instead, providing support and understanding fosters a sense of safety. For example, responding with phrases like, "It's okay to feel that way" or "Thank you for sharing that with me" can make a significant difference. This non-judgmental environment encourages both partners to be their authentic selves, deepening the relationship's emotional intimacy.

By implementing these strategies, couples can foster emotional vulnerability without feeling exposed or insecure. The journey towards deeper emotional connection requires effort and mutual commitment, but the rewards of a more intimate and fulfilling relationship are well worth it.

12.   How can we measure the progress of our relationship without setting unrealistic expectations?

Measuring the progress of a relationship without setting unrealistic expectations involves a balanced approach that combines clear, achievable goals with a flexible mindset. One effective method is establishing shared objectives that both partners agree upon and strive to reach together. These could range from improving communication and spending quality time together to more concrete goals such as financial planning or personal development milestones. By setting realistic and mutually agreed-upon targets, couples can celebrate their progress and have a tangible sense of achievement.

It is equally essential to focus on the process rather than solely on outcomes. This means valuing the efforts and small wins achieved along the way. For instance, if the goal is to communicate better, the focus should be on the incremental improvements in how partners understand and respond to each other, not just on reaching a state of perfect communication. This process-oriented approach reduces pressure and allows for more organic growth within the relationship. It also acknowledges that progress might be non-linear, with potential setbacks serving as learning opportunities rather than failures.

Regular check-ins and open discussions about relationship

dynamics can also serve as a barometer for progress. Partners can set aside time periodically to discuss their feelings about the relationship, any challenges they face, and areas where they feel progress has been made. These conversations should be approached openly and non-judgmentally, ensuring that both partners can speak freely and honestly. This ongoing dialogue helps identify and adjust any unrealistic expectations accordingly, ensuring that the relationship evolves in a healthy and sustainable manner.

Lastly, it is important to celebrate the journey and not just the destination. Acknowledging and appreciating each other's efforts, no matter how small, reinforces positive behavior and motivates both partners to continue striving toward their goals. Shared experiences and creating new memories together also contribute to the relationship's sense of progress and fulfillment. By focusing on everyday moments of connection and support, couples can maintain a sense of continual growth without the pressure of unrealistic expectations.

By implementing these strategies, couples can measure the progress of their relationship in a realistic and supportive manner. The key lies in balancing goal-setting with a flexible and understanding approach, valuing the journey as much as the results, and maintaining open lines of communication. This balanced approach fosters a positive and resilient relationship, enabling partners to confidently grow together and navigate challenges.

13.   What are some simple daily rituals we can incorporate to enhance our connection?

Simple daily rituals can profoundly enhance the connection between partners by creating consistent moments of togetherness and intimacy. These rituals need not be elaborate or time-consuming; rather, they should be activities both partners enjoy and find meaningful. One effective ritual is starting and ending the day together. This could involve sharing a cup of coffee in the morning, discussing the day's plans, or unwinding together in the evening by discussing how the day went. Such moments set a positive tone for the day and help both partners feel connected, even amidst busy schedules.

Another powerful daily ritual is expressing gratitude. Taking a few moments each day to acknowledge and appreciate one another can significantly impact the relationship. This can be as simple as verbally expressing thanks for something the other person did, leaving a thoughtful note, or even sending a quick appreciative text message during the day. Regularly expressing gratitude fosters a positive atmosphere in the relationship, reinforcing feelings of love and appreciation. It also helps partners focus on their relationship's positive aspects, mitigating the impact of everyday stresses and challenges.

Physical touch is another critical component of daily rituals that can enhance connection. Simple gestures such as holding hands, hugging, or cuddling can strengthen the emotional bond between partners. Physical touch has been shown to release oxytocin, often called the "love hormone," which promotes feelings of closeness and reduces stress. Incorporating physical affection into daily interactions helps to maintain a sense of intimacy and reinforces the emotional connection between partners.

Finally, engaging in a shared activity or interest can be a daily ritual that brings partners closer together. This could be cooking a meal together, walking, working on a project or hobby, or setting aside time for a shared reading or movie-watching routine. These activities allow partners to bond over common interests, fostering a sense of teamwork and collaboration. They also provide opportunities for creating shared memories and experiences, which can strengthen the overall foundation of the relationship.

By integrating these simple daily rituals into their routine, couples can significantly enhance their connection and foster a deeper sense of intimacy and partnership. The key is choosing activities that both partners find enjoyable and meaningful, ensuring that these moments become cherished in their daily lives.

14.   How can newly formed couples build a strong foundation using the principles in this book?

Building a strong foundation for a relationship involves creating a basis of trust, open communication, and mutual respect. The principles discussed in this book offer practical strategies to help newly formed couples achieve these goals. One key principle is effective communication. Couples should practice active listening and understand each other's perspectives from the outset. This means hearing the words and paying attention to the underlying emotions and intentions. Establishing clear, honest, and respectful communication helps prevent misunderstandings and builds a foundation of trust and mutual respect.

Another principle is the importance of shared goals and values. Partners should have open discussions about their long-term aspirations and personal values early in the relationship. Identifying common ground can help couples align their objectives and work together towards their goals. This shared vision creates a sense of partnership and mutual support. It also provides a roadmap for making joint decisions and navigating potential conflicts. By understanding and respecting each other's values and aspirations, couples can build a more cohesive and resilient relationship.

As discussed earlier, incorporating daily rituals also plays a crucial role in building a strong foundation. Simple, consistent habits like expressing gratitude, engaging in shared activities, and maintaining physical affection help create a sense of continuity and emotional connection. These rituals enhance the interactions between partners, reinforcing their bond and creating positive experiences to draw upon during challenging times. By prioritizing these small but meaningful acts, couples ensure their relationship remains close-knit and supportive.

Lastly, newly formed couples should focus on developing emotional intelligence. This involves being aware of and managing one's emotions while empathizing with the partner's feelings.

High emotional intelligence facilitates healthier interactions and conflict resolution, as partners are better equipped to handle emotional challenges constructively. By continually working on emotional intelligence, couples can foster a compassionate and understanding environment, which is crucial for a strong and enduring relationship.

By following these principles, newly formed couples can establish a robust foundation for their relationship. Prioritizing effective communication, aligning goals and values, incorporating daily rituals, and developing emotional intelligence create a balanced and nurturing environment. This approach fortifies the relationship in its early stages and sets the stage for a fulfilling and lasting partnership.

15.   How do we handle setbacks or regressions in our relationship progress?

Handling setbacks or regressions in a relationship requires a multi-faceted approach, prioritizing communication, understanding, and resilience. The first step is acknowledging that setbacks are a natural part of any relationship. Recognizing that experiencing difficulties doesn't signify failure but rather an opportunity for growth and learning is crucial. By accepting the inevitability of challenges, couples can approach regressions with a constructive mindset, focusing on finding solutions rather than assigning blame.

Effective communication is fundamental in navigating setbacks.

Both partners need to engage in open and honest conversations when issues arise. This involves active listening, where each person takes the time to understand the other's perspective without interrupting or becoming defensive. Effective communication also means expressing one's feelings and concerns clearly and respectfully. This open dialogue helps identify the root cause of the problem and fosters a cooperative spirit to resolve the issue together. By maintaining transparency and openness, couples can prevent misunderstandings that further exacerbate the situation.

Additionally, cultivating empathy and understanding is essential when dealing with regressions. Each partner should strive to understand not only their own emotions but also their partner's feelings and viewpoints. Empathy allows partners to provide each other with the necessary support and reassurance during challenging periods. Understanding that both individuals may cope differently and require different kinds of support can also help manage expectations and provide emotional backing. This empathetic approach fosters a nurturing environment where both partners feel valued and supported in overcoming setbacks.

Another critical aspect is focusing on solutions and positive actions. Instead of dwelling on the mistakes or problems, couples should focus on finding practical solutions and implementing positive changes. This might involve setting new goals, developing new strategies for managing conflicts, or seeking external support such as couples therapy. Partners can transform setbacks into constructive experiences that strengthen the relationship by working together on actionable steps. Celebrating small victories and progress also helps build momentum and reinforces the partnership's resilience.

Lastly, maintaining a long-term perspective is vital. Relationships are dynamic and ever-evolving, and setbacks are just one part of the journey. By keeping a broader perspective and focusing on the overall growth and development of the relationship, couples can avoid becoming disheartened by temporary setbacks. Viewing challenges as opportunities for growth helps develop a resilient and adaptive partnership. Regularly revisiting shared goals, values, and positive memories can also serve as a reminder of the strength and potential of the relationship, motivating them to weather any storm together.

Thank You

We extend our heartfelt gratitude to you for taking the time to read this book. Your commitment to enhancing your relationship is commendable, and we hope the insights and strategies shared here provide you with valuable guidance.

We believe you can cultivate a more fulfilling and enduring partnership by applying these principles. Thank you for allowing us to join your journey towards a stronger and more resilient relationship.

www.ingramcontent.com/pod-product-compliance
Lightning Source LLC
Chambersburg PA
CBHW051258250726
48656CB00004B/1354